GOD Lucifer, and Me.

How Lucifer tried to seduce me but then I met GOD

Simona Williams

BALBOA.
PRESS
A DIVISION OF HAY HOUSE

Balboa Press books may be ordered through booksellers or by contacting:

Balboa Press
A Division of Hay House
1663 Liberty Drive
Bloomington, IN 47403
www.balboapress.com
1 (877) 407-4847

Because of the dynamic nature of the Internet, any web addresses or links contained in this book may have changed since publication and may no longer be valid. The views expressed in this work are solely those of the author and do not necessarily reflect the views of the publisher, and the publisher hereby disclaims any responsibility for them.

The author of this book does not dispense medical advice or prescribe the use of any technique as a form of treatment for physical, emotional, or medical problems without the advice of a physician, either directly or indirectly. The intent of the author is only to offer information of a general nature to help you in your quest for emotional and spiritual well-being. In the event you use any of the information in this book for yourself, which is your constitutional right, the author and the publisher assume no responsibility for your actions.

Any people depicted in stock imagery provided by Getty Images are models, and such images are being used for illustrative purposes only.
Certain stock imagery © Getty Images.

Print information available on the last page.

Interior Image Credit: William Walker

ISBN: 978-1-9822-3268-9 (sc)
ISBN: 978-1-9822-3267-2 (hc)
ISBN: 978-1-9822-3269-6 (e)

Library of Congress Control Number: 2019911462

Balboa Press rev. date: 08/23/2019

CONTENTS

DEDICATION

I dedicate this book to my beloved father, Alan Hari Levin, who I miss every day, and to whom I would have gladly given up my life for.

Dear Dad, may you have an amazing time with your deceased beloved relatives, animals, and divine angels in heaven.

ACKNOWLEDGEMENTS

This book would not have come to life, nor been written, without the help of my dearest William Walker, who ensured we both worked until it was achieved.

The pictures on the front and back cover of this book are photographed by one of my favorite photographers, Michael Sanville.

The book covers were designed by my good friend, Danielle Brown.

PROLOGUE

I have procrastinated for many years before writing this book. I have been exposed to so many spiritual experiences, that they became normal to me, and just a way of life. I somehow knew that it was important to keep records every time I had an unusual spiritual experience. However, I need to explain, that the contents of this book represent only a part of my total experiences.

I finally put pen to paper in the beginning of 2018, and with the help of a dear friend we started writing this book. As I was doing this, it became clear that important messages were emerging.

I have written carefully, and truthfully, to the best of my ability, about meetings I had with Lucifer (WHO I REFER TO AS 'L') and God, as well as angels and other entities. On several occasions, the encounters were witnessed by other people. It basically came down to this.

We need to recognize that there is an ongoing battle between good and evil. The battle is for our souls. Realize that we always have a choice. A choice to do good or cause harm. It is a waste of time to blame our past, our environment, or other people for our actions.

We can choose not to be a victim, either of circumstances or because we were given hard odds in this life.

We can choose to take control over our life, set goals we wish to achieve, and go for it!

Nothing is impossible if we believe, work hard, and desire something so much that we are willing to fight for it.

The battle I referred to before is about the very balance of good and evil. This balance has been shaken to its core and unfortunately has shifted towards evil.

We, the people on this planet earth are the ones who must change things for the better, and good must flourish.

By writing about Lucifer, and all my experiences with him, I am revealing an important part about evil. Evil, or Lucifer, may come in many disguises. It can be beautiful, attractive, and often desirable and will tempt you to become part of it.

Try to recognize when you are confronting evil by listening to the essence of your soul, located in your solar plexus, it will always warn you. Listen and feel. You will automatically know when something doesn't seem exactly right! Don't give into it!

Listen to your soul. Your soul is God.

It is my responsibility to reveal the truth, based upon my countless spiritual experiences, over the past twenty years. Remember, I am merely the messenger.

HOW GOD COMMUNICATES

It must be said that under no circumstances do I claim any credit for writing this book. Every thought, word and idea, has been channeled through a willful, powerful force called God. My crown chakra opens, and the words come pouring down. I am inundated with a cascade of words, that I either speed write onto a pad, or record into a manual tape recorder, totally unaware of the message content until much later. Sometimes it can be just a couple of pages, other times, as much as twenty, and on some occasions, I have recorded for two hours none stop. I am merely the messenger and write what I am directed. I feel incredibly humbled to be chosen for this task.

FOREWORD

It is a pleasure and privilege to write a few words on behalf of Simona. When she indicated to me in February 2018 that she wanted to write this book, I was happy to volunteer any assistance I could offer. I did this, suspecting, (as I have had some spiritual experience) that as soon as we began, she would come under severe and prolonged spiritual attack, as the messages she had to deliver came directly from God, and exposed the dark side in all its manipulative, ugly ways. Therefore, it came as no big surprise when the challenges hit, like a ton of bricks.

I will list below, some of the things that happened to Simona, and to which I was an ongoing witness, not to illicit sympathy, that is not her way, and certainly not mine, but for the reader to understand the effort, determination, and sheer will power it took to finish this book. She was under no illusions that this book had to be published, come what may, as the messages were too important, and too urgent to accept any delay. As she would put it, "We are literally working against the clock, it is God's will, not mine and I can't let him down. My soul is in pain to finish and publish." It is my fervent hope that the reader will take all of this on board, and realize the tremendous sacrifices Simona has endured, and take the messages to heart.

It is worth pointing out that up to that point, Simona had been very healthy in every way. I may have some of the timing a little out of order, but every one of the listed attacks, took place from February to July 2018.

Immediately we started collating the material, Simona suffered a flare up of a condition she had experienced before, but this time it was much more severe. Normally, she would take medicine and the condition would quickly clear up. This time, the medicine had no effect, so the doctor suggested repeating the dose. Still no improvement, so in desperation she took a third treatment, to no avail, and up to now, her specialist is still looking for answers.

For no apparent reason, she started sleeping for twelve hours, but awoke, still feeling exhausted, and out of the blue daily migraines became the norm, leaving her in a constant state of fatigue. She started living like a hermit, as depression took hold. To make matters worse, if that was at all possible, she also became moody and aggressive.

We all have problems with our teeth from time to time, but with Simona, every possible thing that could have gone wrong, did so. Over a period of weeks, she had all the mercury removed from her fillings as it was poisoning her system. New crowns needed to be fitted, and two very painful root canals had to be addressed, which left her face partially paralyzed, and she lost some sight in one of her eyes. This lasted for days.

Simona is a movie actress, and her face is her passport, so, as you can imagine, when her face started to break out for no reason, she became very concerned. She ordered medication, which mysteriously disappeared, and when a replacement was sent, it acted on her body like poison, making her very ill.

She was hit with a flu virus which took an age to clear, as her immune system was compromised by all the medication she had been taking.

Just as the flu attack began to recede, intestinal Candida set in, causing stomach bloating, more fatigue and pain. Of course, the first medication didn't clear it, and only after a second dose, was it controlled. On the day she decided to devote time to the specific 'God' part of the book, she was overwhelmed with fever and nausea and felt delirious to the point of throwing up. I thought at one point, she would faint.

A bank transaction which should have been simple, was lost in the system, and took hours of painstaking work to figure out the paper trail, and a large heavy mirror, which had been in place for years, suddenly crashed to the floor. Luckily it missed her, as she would have been crushed. As you can imagine, the effects of the continuous attacks, and medication on her body, left her physically debilitated. She was unable to go to the gym, which used to be an almost daily habit, and had difficulty with food, as her system was so compromised and unable to function normally. But despite this, her will was so strong, she wouldn't give up on the project. I have nothing but the utmost respect for her tenacity and perseverance in publishing this book, and I hope you will bear this in mind as you absorb the incredible messages in the following pages.

William H. Walker

GLOSSARY

Please read the following which explains the various terminology used throughout the book.

Out of Body Experience (O.O.B.E.) - Astral Projections

When your soul leaves the body, most of the time you will be able to see your sleeping, physical body still in bed, while you are standing next to it.

You are now pure soul energy, meaning your astral body has separated from your physical body.

You may still feel you have a real body, but it is only energy, not matter.

You are now able to penetrate all matter, which is pure energy, as you are in a different dimension. At this point, you can visit all other dimensions, as they are accessible by penetrating the energy membranes that separate every dimension, of which there are an unlimited number that we are totally unaware of.

The out of body experience is also known as astral projection. When you are only energy, having left your matter, (physical body) you are able to go anywhere. Generally, you don't get to choose where you want to go but are taken by an invisible power.

Personally, I'm always aware when I'm out of my body. In the beginning, and for many years, I used to get 'Christ Energy' that filled every cell in my body with ecstasy. The feeling was indescribable, immediately followed by my astral body levitating to the ceiling. The sensation is beyond amazing.

At this point, being all astral body means you are pure energy, containing all memory, feeling, and awareness, etc. which is the soul. Our soul is part of God.

Now for the fun bit. I would do what I have done for many years, and poke my head through the bedroom wall, that consists of energy, made from constantly vibrating molecules. I knew if my head would go through the wall, my astral body would follow.

I was then able to penetrate all dimensions and have been to more than a hundred of these dimensions. It is important to understand both future and past simultaneously exist.

I have been taken places, that we as humans have no concept of. A great power, that I call God, would take me to the most incredible places. I was shown things beyond imagination. I would also participate in battles that were being fought, and experiences in other dimensions that were simply mind blowing. I have been to heaven, hell, other planets, seen strange creatures, and other beings; all of this co-exists with our world. I have met with God, Lucifer, angels, demons, other creatures and extra-terrestrials

THE MIDDLE STAGE

The middle stage is a very significant factor in an out of body experience. When you are in this stage, you can recognize what's going on around you as well as what is happening to you.

In my case, this stage occurs right before I wake up (and become fully conscious). I am now as close to being conscious as I can be, without being fully awake.

In this stage, I can hear and see things in my bedroom, such as sounds from other people, doors opening and closing, etc. as well as supernatural phenomena.

This is the perfect stage at which I can leave my physical body and use my astral body to immediately enter another dimension.

You may also find yourself standing in what appears at first to be your own bedroom, but what in fact is another dimension. You are now able to see all the energy in every molecule floating around in your room, continually moving and constantly changing. Everything is now a vibration of energy.

CHAPTER 1

Growing Up In Denmark

I was born and grew up in Denmark, in what I would define as a normal family life, with a wonderful mother and father. I recall I always had cats and I guess I have been attracted to animals as far back as I can recall. Something about their purity and innocence always appealed to me. I loved all animals, and when I was seven, I started horseback riding and soon owned two horses of my very own. They became a very important part of my life, as indeed, to this day, every animal is very important to me.

Even though I grew up in a normal family, my life was far from normal. My school years were a living hell. I was always the outsider, and never felt I belonged. I attended five different schools growing up, as my parents moved frequently, and in every single school, I was bullied constantly, from the age of seven until I was fifteen. Severe bullying became part of my life. I was beaten

1

up several times a week, usually after school, and kept out of all group activities. I was verbally abused, and belittled by the girls in my class, and after lunch break, they would throw water at me, soaking my hair and clothes. So, to say that my school days were normal would be far from the truth.

I've since tried to figure out why I was bullied so much, and eventually came up with one possible reason. I believe that anyone who is seen to be "different," in any way is a prime target for bullying, and in my case, I think it was because I was a pretty little girl. I had long, dark hair down to my waist, and boys liked me. Also, I became aware later, that other girls saw me different to them, and as one girl put it, I looked kind of translucent. I never quite understood that.

At the age of fifteen, I was accepted into a modeling agency, and started doing a lot of print modeling. As you can imagine, that did not go well with the girls. I could feel the envy when I entered the classroom. I attended college eventually, at my father's insistence, and I continued to law school, where after five years, I passed my exams and achieved a Juris Doctor degree in law, which is the equivalent of passing the bar exam in the U.S.

A defining moment in my life was when I was fourteen. My parents took me on a trip to California. They were visiting friends who had migrated there several years earlier. They had two daughters who were both my friends. The older daughter and I became best friends and being the adventurous types, we decided we wanted to go to nightclubs in Hollywood, where everything was happening.

It was a very exciting idea, but there was a problem. We weren't old enough to gain access, but we quickly managed to find a way to get past the bouncers by greasing their palms with lots of crinkly notes. We had a blast. This left me with a strong feeling, deep inside, that this was the place I eventually wanted to live.

From that moment on, I made it my mission to spend as much time as possible in California. Every chance I got, mainly during school holidays, I would jump on a plane and high tail it to California.

While I was studying at law school, and making regular trips to Hollywood, I became friends with some prominent movie people and managed to secure a talent manager in Los Angeles. I was determined to become a recognized actress. I loved acting. It was and still is an irresistible passion of mine.

Later, I realized my interest in acting had started at a very early age. I was seven when a friend and I built a theater out of cardboard boxes and put on a play. We both acted our parts, but of course, I was the director. I was bitten by the acting bug and used every opportunity to act. It was a wonderful escape from my everyday life of bullying.

While I was in Denmark, I started to take acting lessons from a very prominent acting teacher, at the New Theater in Copenhagen, studying Chekhov, and soon, every time I visited California, I would also take lessons from the best teachers around.

The extensive acting training paid dividends, as it wasn't long before I was offered parts in movies, and of course, I eventually moved to Los Angeles to pursue my movie career.

One of the reasons I am exposing my life to you, especially the many unhappy years when I was mercilessly bullied, is to show you that it doesn't matter where you start; it's where you finish. The choices we make on our individual journey, determines where we finish up. We all have choices. Follow your dream and your passions, no matter what obstacles are in your way. Never become a victim. Your dreams are yours and nobody else's. They belong to you, and only you can make them happen, or prevent them from happening. Choose wisely.

Finally, I need to address one question which I know will be asked on a regular basis. Why me? Why was I chosen to be bombarded with visits from "L" and exposed to the most indescribable experiences imaginable. It was certainly not because I was religious. My father was half Jewish, but never paid any attention to the faith, as in Denmark, the social culture is not particularly religiously inclined. I never attended church or any religious festivals, and my parents never suggested that I did. I do remember that in fifth grade at school, there were bible classes as part of the curriculum, but I mostly skipped them and never knew much about the bible and didn't really care, so I was puzzled why Lucifer wanted me to know him, and took an interest in me, or more specifically my soul.

My strong belief is that part of the reason I was chosen, was to complete God's task that had to do with a promise I made to Him on a soul level.

Color Blind

Growing up in Denmark, neither me, my friends or family would ever defer to a person because of the color of their skin.

I had many friends, and one of my especially good friends was a disc jockey in Copenhagen. Everybody knew him. I remember telling my parents that "I'm bringing home a friend for dinner." It never occurred to me to refer to him as an African American, neither did I describe him as an African American to my parents or friends, because it did not matter.

To me, he was simply a person, like everyone else, and should never be referred to by his skin color, because who cares, we are all children of God and should be treated as such, regardless of our skin color, heritage or cultural background.

I want to elaborate on this subject by giving an example of what I realized was taking place in the U.S.A.

While I was still residing in Denmark, and attending school, I took countless trips to L.A. whenever I got the chance. On one of these trips, I met one of the most beautiful girls I have ever seen.

She had long hair, an incredible agile and slender body, and the most amazing smile. We became friends for many years and were inseparable. She was my best girlfriend in L.A. We did everything together, whether it was putting on our makeup, going for acting auditions, or partying.

Then I started dating a guy with blue eyes and blonde hair who happened to be in the acting industry. I stayed in his apartment when I was in L.A. which was quite often. The incident that I will now describe has stayed with me as a vivid, horrendous memory since then.

His parents came into town and invited us out for late lunch. I asked my boyfriend if I could bring my best girlfriend along, whom he had never met, and he said no problem. We all met up at a restaurant in Santa Monica. My girlfriend arrived a little late and joined the group and I thought we had a great time. I purposefully placed her next to me, as she didn't know anyone, and when we were done, my girlfriend took off, as she had errands to do. Having said goodbye to his parents, my boyfriend pulled me aside. I will never forget the words that came out of his mouth. "Simona I really don't think she fits in with our circle of friends."

As you can imagine, the relationship did not last long after that, as I really valued my girlfriend's friendship.

CHAPTER 2

Spirit In The Glass

During my college years in Denmark, and while 'L' continued to visit me, I became curious about a game called 'Spirit in the Glass.' I would get together with a group of friends, usually at my home, which was a large mansion my father had built. We would meet there and sit around a table in the large room where the indoor pool was located, and play.

On one occasion, I remember my brother and I were there, along with my best friend and her boyfriend, plus a couple of others. I would cut out all the letters of the Danish alphabet and place them on the table, then put a small glass in the center. I must point out that it was not a Ouija board, which has numbers, letters, a sun and moon. It was a simple game that had no negative energies, or so I thought. It was just a game we had made up to experiment with. Nevertheless, I would not recommend you try this at home.

Either with the game, or anything similar, as there are inherent dangers that a portal can be unwittingly opened. You can never be sure what might show up, and once a portal is opened, it is very difficult to close.

Anyway, to return to the story, here we all were, sitting around the table playing a game that I had played many times before. We were all so curious to see what, if anything, might happen. We all placed a finger on the glass, and as usual, it began to move, even before we had time to ask any questions, which was unusual. Normally, it would not move until a question had been asked. But on this occasion, it began to spell out the same thing over and over. "I love you, Simona. I love you, Simona."

My friends became frustrated and annoyed with this, so we decided to test the authenticity of the message. We discussed how we could do it and were struggling to decide, when my mother approached. Suddenly, one of my friends had a bright idea. "Let's ask your mom to help," she said. My mother, of course, always keen to join in, agreed. "What do you want to do?" she said. "I know," I said. "Can you go to the library and choose any book at random and bring it back here? But don't tell us the title." My mother agreed and headed off towards the library. She returned within a few minutes and stood at the far end of the pool, some thirty yards away, with the book in her hand. We could barely make out that it was a book she was holding, and we certainly couldn't see the title.

(See footnote 1)

We all placed our fingers back on the glass and asked the spirit to name the book my mother was holding. The glass started to move and spelt out *The Orient Express*. Not totally satisfied, I asked the glass to repeat the title and once more the glass spelt out *The Orient Express*. I thought "Wow, that's interesting," and asked my mother to come over to the table and hold up the book. Sure enough, it was *The Orient Express*. I thought it was way cool, but everyone else freaked out, including my mother, when she realized what had just happened.

It was obvious to everyone that something at the table was communicating with us. I didn't know at the time, but later realized it was 'L.' Years later, my mother told me that as she stood at the far end of the pool room, near the bar, she heard a low growling, animalistic noise. She remembers it so well, even though it was years ago.

As we all sat there trying to figure out what had just happened, one of my friends pointed at the table and gasped, "Look, it's horns." (See footnote 2) We all stared at the table in disbelief. Sure enough, appearing right in front of our eyes were goat's horns. Nobody really wanted to believe it, so we moved the candles around and adjusted the lights, but it wasn't a cast shadow. It was very real. It was a pair of goat horns. For absolute confirmation, I asked my mother, who had wandered off, to come take a look. "Oh my God," she exclaimed. "It's goat's horns." We discussed the phenomena at length, and speculated it might be 'L,' but it wasn't until later that I knew the truth. It was 'L.'

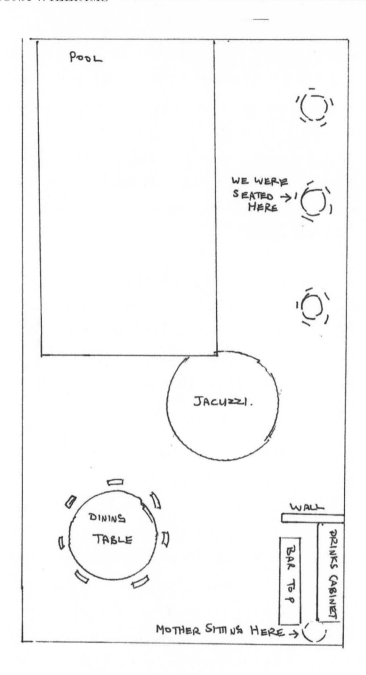

Footnote 1

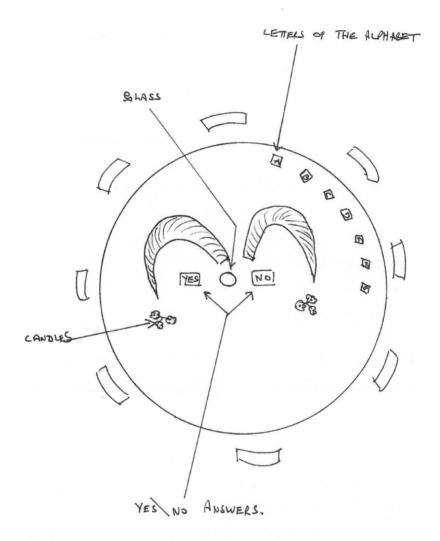

SPIRIT IN THE GLASS TABLE SHOWING GOAT HORNS.

LETTERS OF THE ALPHABET

GLASS

YES NO

CANDLES

YES NO ANSWERS.

Footnote 2

Two months later, I drove from my home, which is about twenty minutes from Copenhagen, into the city to meet two of my friends. By this time, we were all very curious about the 'Spirit in the Glass' game and wanted to find out what messages might come through. You would think that after what had happened the last time, we wouldn't want to repeat the experiment. But curiosity got the best of us, and we decided to play the game.

There were about eight of us in total, so in no time at all, we had cut out all the letters, and arranged them on the table. A glass was placed in the center and we all nervously touched our fingers on top of the glass. Before any questions could be asked, the glass started to move. It spelt out, "I will say hi." I was so excited that I was first to speak. "Oh, my God, guys, it wants to say hi!" The glass spelt out once more, "I will say hi." Again, I spoke up. "That's so cool! It wants to say hi."

The moment the words left my mouth, a loud, growling, vile, animalistic sound, coming from nothing human, filled the room.

As the sound continued, my friends freaked out. One girl, hysterical, rushed to the window and tried to climb out. Luckily, it was locked, which prevented her from jumping out. The flat was on the third floor and it wouldn't have ended well. The rest of my friends panicked and fled for the door, desperate to escape. During all the chaos, I suddenly realized I was still sitting at the table, and for some reason, not in the least bit scared. In fact, I thought it was so cool and couldn't understand why my friends had reacted so crazily. It took me quite a while to calm everyone down. They'd had the fright of their lives and couldn't understand why I wasn't scared.

My mother had a similar experience a couple of weeks later. Although, on that occasion, there was no 'Spirit in the Glass' involved. She was visiting a friend in Copenhagen who had organized a get together with a bunch of girlfriends. As they were sitting chatting in the friends' apartment, a horrific, loud growling sound filled the room. Everyone froze at the vile sound, when suddenly, from outside on the street, they heard a loud crash. Everyone rushed to the window. Below them, two cars had collided at the precise time the vile sound had started. The coincidence was too striking to ignore, and it took a long while for everyone to get over it.

After my mother had witnessed a number of these alarming experiences, she decided that something should be done about it and arranged to have our home spiritually cleansed. She contacted a spiritual friend and asked her to help. Her friend readily agreed and eventually arrived, bringing with her a boyfriend, sea salt, sage, and a collection of herbs to use in the ceremony.

They began in the pool room, which appeared to be the site where most unusual activities had taken place. My mother and her friend started walking around the edge of the pool, which had been emptied, to allow for repair work. As they approached the deepest part, my mother's friend suddenly lunged forward as if she had been pushed. Of course, there was no one there. At least no one visible. My mother frantically reached out and grabbed her in the nick of time, preventing her friend from plunging into the empty pool and cracking her skull upon the tiles.

It then became apparent to them both that they were dealing with dangerous invisible forces, well beyond the scope of most people's imaginations. My mother and her friend were badly shaken by the experience but became even more determined to continue with the spiritual cleansing. As they moved from room to room, my mother's friend told her that there were evil entities everywhere in the house, especially in the bedroom, just lingering. The spiritual healer proceeded to scatter sea salt, and burn sage, systematically throughout the house, until she felt it was clear. I think the sea salt, herbs and sage were useful, as it appeared that the space had been cleansed.

For a while, the house was clean, but, as I realized later, every time I exercised my curiosity with the 'Spirit' game, I was allowing more infestation. But for me at the time, as the entities did me no harm, and I certainly didn't fear them. I continued, and in fact, began to feel a kind of weird friendship towards them.

Another experience my mother had, when I was still present in the house, occurred one night when she was in bed, but not quite asleep. She described a feeling I had experienced many times. She felt the duvet being lifted, but at the same time, felt someone walking on it. Then she heard her name being called, over and over again. This woke her from the middle stage into total consciousness, that is, fully awake. She peered around the bedroom, but no one was there.

Very recently, in fact as I was writing this book, my mother called me from Spain and told me something weird had happened. She described how she was lying in bed, not fully awake. She was in the middle stage, just before waking, when she felt her legs were being bound together and pushed down into the mattress. She desperately wanted to wake up and lose the awful feeling of being held down against her will, but instead, she heard a male voice calling her. She believed it was one of my brothers saying, "I miss you. I miss you." Suddenly she became fully conscious and desperately searched the room, but there was no one there. When she told me this, I explained to her I didn't believe my brother was able to leave his body to be with her. It wasn't my brother, it was 'L', playing his vile tricks. He comes in many disguises, changing his appearance at will, and can assume any voice he chooses.

Surprisingly enough, I continued playing the 'Spirit in the Glass' game, even though I suspected it was a dumb decision. My curiosity was insatiable, especially since a while back I had discovered that the glass would move, the second I touched it, whether I was with other people or alone.

By then I had moved to Los Angeles and was taking the game seriously; to the extent that I found a piece of wood and marked the letters on it with a marker pen. So there I was, alone in my apartment in L.A. with the glass and letters in front of me, eager to start the game. I placed two fingers on the glass, which immediately started to move. I could ask any questions I liked, and I would receive an answer, but most of the time, I simply asked what it wanted to tell me. It would form full sentences of a predictive nature, which would always come true. I was absolutely amazed by some of the things I learned, but eventually began to realize that I was being led into a trap. I was being enticed to use it more and more and become very familiar with the spirit. It was, of course, 'L' who wanted to gain free access to me, which by the way, I never gave him.

So back to the story. I was touching the glass, when out of the blue I received a message. "You will get a part in a movie in April." My first thought was "No way, not a chance in hell, I'll be in Spain. No one will bother to contact me then, even if they could find me." But the message repeated several times, so for once, I decided to write it down. I thought no more about it, until a little while later while at my parent's house in Spain, I received a phone call from a movie company I had worked for previously. They wanted me to go to Bulgaria where they had a part for me. I was totally shocked as I recalled the prediction that the 'Spirit in the Glass' had made. It was in April, exactly as it had said. I had no idea how the movie company had tracked me down, as to my knowledge, they didn't have my number in Spain. I packed my bags, flew to Sophia in Bulgaria and shot the movie.

I returned to L.A. with the movie behind me, now even more curious to continue with the game, but being cautious, I decided to visit a spiritual book- store in West Hollywood, thinking I should buy an Angel Board. My thought process was that I would be talking to angels, not demons, which was a much more positive force.

I started playing with my new game and a couple of girlfriends joined in. The second I touched the plastic planchette, it moved with incredible speed. So much so, that my friends had to stand back to read the sentences. Most of the time the information that came through was very accurate, but eventually, after playing a while, the tone changed. It started becoming very personal, which I knew was not good, saying things like "I love you. We used to be together. You were my wife. Don't choose God, choose me. I'm the only one who loves you." I knew of course, that it was 'L.' He persisted with these messages and kept on asking me, "Please open the portal." At this point, I realized I was being sucked into a dangerous situation and stopped playing the game. There is no way I would ever think about opening a portal. No freaking way.

If for any reason you haven't gotten the message by now, let me re-emphasize. Ouija boards, angel boards or any type of board, are not just harmless party games. They must be taken very seriously. They are a potential way that evil can invade your soul and do irreparable harm. Especially if you allow a portal to be opened. Even if you are totally unaware of what you are doing, the consequences can be dire. If ever you are drawn, by curiosity, or any other motives, to tamper with the spiritual world, be warned. Evil is just waiting for its chance to insinuate its way into your life. Never, under any circumstances, agree to open a portal, no matter how tempting the request might appear at the time.

CHAPTER 3

Tarot Cards, Voodoo, Ghosts

My time with the 'Spirit in the Glass' came to an end, but my insatiable curiosity remained intact, so I turned my attention to tarot cards. My mother had studied the subject and spent time with tarot cards, after researching the subject. She had cute cards, so of course, I went looking. Unfortunately, I bought the wrong set of cards, which I didn't discover until later. Despite the minor setback, I found I could still read them like there was no tomorrow. It came easy to me. Even if I didn't know what a card meant, I was channeled through and able to read it. When I read for someone, my success rate was 99%. I could give times, dates, places, and predictions. In fact, everything there was to know about the subject, with almost total accuracy.

Later, I learnt I was playing with Aleister Crowley, an occult worshipper's cards, but I believed that Lady Frieda Harris, the lady who painted the cards, was a good soul. Initially, the cards worked well, but eventually, similar to my experience with the 'Spirit in the Glass,' the tone changed. I would repeatedly shuffle the deck, but the ten worst cards would always come out. So, I bought a new deck and surprise, surprise, the same thing happened. They started out great, giving very accurate information, but soon turned bad, so I had no choice but to destroy them. As a precaution, I cleansed my apartment with sage and holy water, although it probably wasn't necessary.

I must make it clear at this point, that my experiments with the 'Spirit in the Glass' and tarot cards was born from my intense desire to meet and talk to God. Now, with the 'Spirit in the Glass' and tarot cards out of my life, I was afraid their disappearance would leave a vacuum. I needn't have worried. My out of body experiences and channeling which are much more rewarding and simply amazing, continued!

My Voodoo Experience

My spiritual journey has taken me down many paths, mainly driven by intense curiosity, but there is one experience I was in no way curious about. It just happened.

I was in a great mood and had been for a while. The main reason for my euphoria was that with the help of a friend, I had secured a huge part in a new movie called *Sumuru*. I was to play the part of an evil snake goddess called *Taxan*. We were scheduled to do the shoot in Johannesburg, and I was very excited, as I had never been to South Africa before.

After a long, and exhausting flight from L.A., I finally arrived at my destination where I was picked up by an assigned driver who would chauffeur me for the entire three weeks of the shoot, which was amazing. We arrived at the five star hotel I was staying in and taken to one of the most beautiful suites I had ever seen.

We started filming, and as the days were long and exhausting, I couldn't wait to get back to my suite for a good night's sleep.

One night, as I was lying in bed, trying to sleep, as I had a very early start the next day, I suddenly saw something I had never encountered before. A solid, black mass, almost two feet wide hovered above my bed, close to my face, making certain I was aware it was there.

It was dark in the bedroom, but the mass was so black, I could still see it clearly. It quickly took on the shape of a horrifying evil face. It looked very real. This annoyed me, as I had to be up very early, and didn't appreciate the ugly, black face in front of me, trying to keep me awake. I told it to get lost and gave it the finger before turning over and sleeping.

Talking to some of the crew later, they said it was probably voodoo, something I was totally unfamiliar with. The next night, the face appeared again, and once more I told it in no uncertain terms to go, before turning over and going to sleep. The stupid, idiotic face kept on appearing night after night until most likely, it got tired of my total lack of respect for it and lack of fear. Finally, it gave up and vanished.

Ghosts In My Bedroom

Most people are familiar with the phenomenon of ghosts. Many have never experienced this and are skeptical about the concept, especially if they haven't had a personal experience.

There are numerous books, T.V. shows, and movies about these mysterious entities, and of course as you may have guessed by now, I had my own experience which I will now relate.

While I was living in L.A., I used to wake up regularly early in the morning and turn over in bed. As I moved my head, I was aware of a lot of movement in the right-hand corner of my bedroom. I watched this strange apparition for at least ten minutes before I realized I was looking at ghosts. They came close to my bed and I counted at least twenty. They were all around three feet tall, with different looks. Some were dumpy, some slimmer and all an opaque gray color. They were not human in appearance, but had heads, necks, legs and arms which they would beat up and down in the air. They seemed angry, but most of all frustrated and in despair. I felt they were miserable. This continued for a couple of years. They were always present in the corner of my bedroom.

Every morning I awoke they were there and eventually I became annoyed seeing them. They were so angry and miserable, that I gave them the finger and told them to get out, so I could go back to sleep. It so happened that at that time, my mother and her friend Ulla were visiting me, and when Ulla entered my bedroom for the first time, she took one look in the corner and said, "Simona, are you aware that you have an open portal in the corner and I can see a lot of ghosts lingering there, but they are not human-like. They are completely trapped. They come from the Hollywood hills through an underground portal that leads directly to your bedroom. You are not supposed to have any open portals, so I'll close it for you."

Since that day, I experienced no more activity in that corner.

Looking back on this experience, I realized something important. Instead of giving them the finger and telling them to go, I should have shown more compassion, especially since I now understand that they were miserable and possibly seeking my help. Instead of dismissing them, I should have tried to help, even if it meant getting outside assistance.

My Beloved Gay Friends

Ever since I was fourteen years old, living in Denmark, I would visit gay clubs. For me it was not unusual, as Denmark is an open culture and very tolerant.

I felt very comfortable around gay men and women, even though I am a straight female, and they felt comfortable around me. Later, when I moved to L.A. my favorite places to go were the gay clubs in West Hollywood. I even continued after I got married, as I had much more fun around gay people than going to boring straight clubs. At one point, I was good friends with 25 gay men and women, as compared to my two straight friends.

My reason for my infatuation with the gay community and clubs was because of their passion for living. They are the most fun people to be around, with the most sarcastic sense of humor, which I totally appreciate. They also happen to have impeccable taste in clothing and makeup, and were totally dedicated to choosing my outfits, and putting on my makeup when we went out clubbing. They totally wanted me to be a diva, and I enjoyed every second of it. We would dance all night and have the time of our lives. I have never received so many compliments as when I went out to gay clubs. All my friends knew they could trust me, and I gained their confidence. They knew I would never betray them.

As they began confiding more and more in me about their lives, and seeking my advice, I started helping them by tuning into their energy and finding solutions for their problems. Most of them knew I was able to do tarot cards and wanted me to give them readings.

On many occasions, when I went to my favorite gay clubs, I would randomly go to people, tune into their energy and tell them things about their lives, which they could not understand how I possibly could have known.

On one occasion, something very unusual happened. I went up to a gay man, a complete stranger, who was standing by himself in an outside area. Even though there were other people around him, and loud music could be heard, I knew he felt isolated. I grabbed his arm and asked him what was wrong. He looked at me in a very weird way and told me straight out he was going to commit suicide that night.

For the next twenty minutes, I got into a huge debate with him, trying to tell him in every possible way, how this was completely unnecessary. Then he did something, which to this day, I shall never forget. He said out loud, "No matter what you say, I'm still doing it." Then he blew on my face as he said, "Here, I give you my last breath." As soon as he had done this, he ran towards the exit and out of the club, leaving me completely dumbfounded.

When my friends eventually found me, after 45 minutes of searching, they were pretty pissed off with me, as I had just disappeared. It took me a while to get over this traumatic event, and I still wonder what happened to that guy.

CHAPTER 4

Lucifer

It is difficult for me to recall the precise day when all this started, and my life was changed forever, when everything I knew as normal, was challenged from all angles, but I remember it was when I was fourteen and living in Denmark, and 'L' paid me a visit.

I was in the middle stage, which I described earlier in this book, but there is no harm repeating the description here. The best way to understand is to imagine the specific moment, just before you wake up, when you're not fully asleep but not quite awake. This is the moment I refer to as 'the middle stage.'

There are many phenomenon, which all take place in the 'middle stage,' such as out of body experiences, or when you have a vivid dream and you can't shake it off. At other times, you may have felt you weren't alone in the room, even when you knew no one was there, or felt something holding you down.

My first experience started in the middle stage, and it would always be the same way in many subsequent visits. On this occasion, I felt a presence lifting the duvet. I could feel the cold air enter as it was lifted. Then I would feel a human presence as a body crawled under the duvet, right next to me. For a short period of time, I was unable to open my eyes and look at him, because I knew it was a 'him.'

I learned by using nothing but sheer will power, I could force my eyes open to look at the presence. There he was, a masculine, overly handsome, dark haired man, staring directly into my eyes. I was absolutely captivated by this image. The scenario continued to happen again and again, over a period of years. The initial experience wasn't at all frightening for me. I was more curious about the strange but very handsome presence. He didn't touch me, just looked at me. But eventually, when I realized who, or what he really was, I became aware that what he really wanted was my soul. He wanted me to love him, and only him, which would mean having to surrender my soul, which I could never do. My soul belongs to God, and always will. Maybe that's why 'L' found me so desirable, or should I say, my soul so desirable. To this day, he has not given up, although his appearances have become less and less frequent.

I guess I was allowed these experiences to teach me just how devious, clever, and insidiously evil 'L' can be, and he never gives up. As we have choices, he will insist we use them. It's part of the battle for souls.

Carried To The Couch

I have had many experiences with 'L,' far too many to include in this book, but this one stands out because of the fear and the absolute dread I felt. Usually, I am not afraid of 'L,' but rather, more curious, so this was alarming, and I remember how I felt at the time, and still to this day, even though it was many years ago.

I was at my parent's home in Denmark, in my private section, with its own bedroom, and found myself once again in the middle stage. My physical body was still in bed, but I was looking at it from the center of the bedroom. As I stood there, I gradually became aware that I was in an entirely different dimension.

The room and the air within it were all vibrating. I could watch the particles moving back and forth with incredible speed. There were no physically solid objects. Everything was energy and vibrations. There was no sound, but the effect on my senses was unimaginable. At the forefront of my feelings were fear and dread. I did not want to be there under any circumstances. I knew I was about to encounter something evil. The fear increased as I moved toward the bedroom door, which I was aware was there, even though I knew it was not solid. But I felt strongly that I had to get out.

I opened the door and sprinted towards my private living room, desperately seeking a way out. Suddenly, I tripped, even though there was nothing in my way, and fell headlong. Without warning, I felt myself being lifted effortlessly and carried forward like a little baby. My fear intensified as I knew it was 'L'. Something was about to happen that would shake me to the core.

I was gently placed on the couch, with my head facing away. I knew that I wasn't supposed to look at him. Then I heard a voice. It was deep, dark and very scary. Certainly not of this world. The best way that I can begin to describe how I felt after hearing that voice is if you can imagine the absolute scariest movie you have ever seen and magnify it ten times. Then you might get some idea, but even that doesn't scratch the surface. It's a voice that will stay with me forever.

It spoke in a language so ancient that it came from somewhere before time began. And although it was a terrifying sound, behind it I felt a loving essence. The whole episode left me feeling deeply disturbed. Not just by the voice, but the fact that I wasn't allowed to see him. The next thing I knew, I was back in my bed, regaining full consciousness with the experience vividly etched in my mind and psyche. It took me weeks, months, to get over it, and it still haunts me today

'L's Energy Membrane Seduction

Ever since I was fourteen, 'L' had made incredible steps in his efforts to seduce my soul. The following is one of his attempts to impress me.

Once again, I was not quite asleep, but not fully awake. I was in the middle stage. I felt the covers lifting and knew 'L' was there. Suddenly I was looking at a large energy membrane, a round sphere of moving molecules I could see through. I had to force open my eyes to peer through them. Then I saw something truly astonishing. It was 'L,' as handsome as ever, his head leaning to one side. Then I saw myself in the membrane, leaning my head toward him. But something was different. I was looking at a younger me, a rounder face, and thicker eyebrows. As I gazed at this romantic picture, I could tell that 'L' had created it for me, to remind me of the infatuation I used to have for him, and the love he still has for me. As the membrane dissolved, I realized he was trying to make me remember that he still loved me and wouldn't let me go.

It was a striking vision, and in many ways, very disturbing. When I awoke into full consciousness, I tried to make sense of it all. The conclusion I reached was that 'L' will use every trick in the spiritual book to gain possession of a soul. The harder a soul clings to God, the more effort 'L' will make to win it over, and he will never stop. Why would he? In the world of the soul, there is no such thing as time.

A Demon Visits Me In L.A.

There were many occasions when 'L' visited me, but this time stands out. I was living in L.A. and had been visiting my parents in Denmark. I had returned to L.A. to continue my acting career and be with my boyfriend.

One night, we were both in bed and he had drifted off, when I became aware that I was in the middle stage. I felt the all too familiar disturbance as the bed covers began to lift. I had encountered this phenomenon many times before, and I knew I was about to enter a state of out of body experience. I clearly felt myself exiting my body and moving to the center of the room. This was not the first time I had left my body, but this was different. I felt weightless and not constrained by gravity as I stood in the middle of the bedroom. It's almost impossible to describe the feeling. It is the most awesome experience imaginable. I felt completely weightless, free to travel anywhere, in any direction, unaffected by the usual laws of physics as we understand them. It is beyond description. It is total freedom, the ultimate truth. I had become an astral body.

As I looked around, I could tell I was in another dimension. Everything around me was shimmering energy, containing a myriad of colors I had never seen before. I could see the gaps between the molecules as they vibrated. Simply amazing.

Then a strong knowing came over me that there was a bad presence waiting for me in the next room. I couldn't see the into the room, I just knew that's where the presence waited. I didn't want to go there at all, and I resisted, but then an invisible force lifted me and pushed me at high speed into the other room.

As I entered, I was overwhelmed by a sense of pure evil. The whole room felt evil. The next thing I knew, I was face to face with a demon. Not just face to face but literally nose to nose, only inches apart. As I looked at the evil demon, I had no fear, just a feeling of power and strength.

Without warning, I felt myself levitate three feet into the air, and as this was happening, I felt huge, white, feathery wings pop out from behind me. I spoke to the demon in a voice I knew wasn't mine. The voice was neither male nor female, but endowed with powerful authority. "You have to leave." The demon laughed in my face and said "No, I'm not leaving." I felt absolutely no fear as I said "Yes, you have to leave because I'm stronger than you, I have wings, and I'm closer to God. God is with me. You don't stand a chance."

The second these words were spoken, a powerful bright golden light, coming from behind me, filled the room. Immediately the demon disappeared. The next thing I remember, I was back in my body regaining full consciousness. When I returned to my body, and became part of the world again, a wave of disappointment descended on me. This dimension sucked big time!

I have visited many different dimensions, but there are many more to experience. I will be sharing a lot of these further in the book, but it is worth explaining at this point that the dimensions I have been to so far, whether I was encountering evil or God, are way above our limited imagination, and it is almost impossible to describe them. There are colors, unknown to us, so vivid and powerful. Everything that ever was, or will be, exists in these other dimensions, far beyond our capacity to understand. In this dimension, we are constrained by time, gravity and matter, imposing human rules and regulations to control our human instincts, what we believe in, and how we interact with each other.

If it was my choice, I would choose all these other dimensions, simply rummaging around all of them, having a blast. I really don't like being in this human dimension.

Finally, I can't leave this chapter without expanding just a little on levitation. It is the most awesome thing I have ever experienced. There is no gravity, nothing holding me back, just an unseen powerful force lifting me up. The amazing thing is, I can stop whenever I choose. Usually I am in another dimension when this occurs. There are literally countless other dimensions, but one in particular is where evil is present. When I'm in this dimension, I know I'm there for a reason; to defeat evil, and the most amazing thing happens, which I don't pretend to understand. Out of nowhere, huge, white feather wings appear on my back. For some reason, I know that God is helping me. I'm not saying I'm an angel, but I do feel an angel entering my body. I totally understand that in my human form I can't have wings, but in other dimensions, I feel an angel presence merging into my body. The presence is more female than male, and I know it's an archangel. There is no way to describe the feeling of the wings on my back; such incredible power and authority. I know it's me in one sense, but I'm also aware it's not me. It's as if we are two in one. She is entering my body, but I am in her dimension. When I speak, I feel it's her speaking, but still me. The overall feeling is way above sensational. I wish I could be in that state all of the time because it is awesome. I have no idea why she has chosen to help me. I can only presume it's with God's blessing.

The Devil's Den

One of the many challenges I faced when having out of body experiences was how to access other dimensions. On most occasions, someone, or something would take me, but I wanted to do it myself. So, after experimenting, I discovered that I could test the situation by sticking my head into the membrane. If my head went through, then it was ok for my body to follow. This next experience is one such case.

I was in my bedroom, sometime during July 2008, when I remember leaving my body. I was perfectly aware that I was out of my body and couldn't wait to test the membrane. I stuck my head into the membrane and went straight through. I was astral energy. I found myself standing in a long hallway, in a different dimension. It was very dim, so I slowly moved forward until I ended up in a small room, which had dark, velvet curtains. I realized I was in 'L's' den. As I looked around, I could see many high- backed chairs, made from some black material, positioned in a circle. I couldn't tell what, if anything was in the center of the circle, but I could see there were people sitting in the chairs as if everything was normal. I said, "Why are you guys here?" One of them answered "We have chosen to be here, but now we are regretting this choice because we are stuck in the chairs and unable to move." I felt extremely sorry for all these people. I turned around and walked towards a huge mirror and looked at the reflection. I was shocked. Looking back at me was a blonde- haired young boy of around seven years old. It was made obvious to me, the only way to gain access to 'L's' private quarters, especially in this case, was by disguising myself as a young boy. Only then would I be able to speak to the people in the circle without being found out, or so I thought.

I saw my reflection, and looked up, very much aware of a strong presence. It was 'L,' right in front of me. He confronted me and started teasing me, putting me down. Totally forgetting that I appeared to him as a young boy, I asked him, "Are you afraid of me?" 'L' laughed out loud and said, "No." 'L's' laughter must have triggered something, because suddenly I felt myself growing into a presence with large, white wings. I looked 'L' straight in the eyes, and this time, in a deep, powerful voice, totally devoid of any fear, I said "You should be afraid of me because I have God behind me." Immediately, a bright golden light shone from behind me and 'L' withdrew right away. Yet again, I had proved my faith in God and we had won.

T.V. Show – 'L' Annoyed

By now, I guess you will have realized that 'L' will go to any lengths if he feels threatened, or his seductions are not working. One such example is when I decided to pitch a T.V. show about spirituality and of course he appeared.

I believe, if my memory serves me correctly, that around June 23rd, 2013, I contacted my dear friend, Darlene King, also known as The Barrington Medium, to discuss pitching a T.V. show that would include such things as out of body experiences. We knew if the show was picked up by one of the major networks, it would be a huge hit. Darlene is not just a medium, contacting those already passed over, but also a healer, so we were very excited.

That evening when I went to bed, I entered a dream state that was so vivid that I didn't know if I was out of my body or dreaming. I experienced entering a large white house, that I knew was mine. It was clear to me right then that I was in the future. I was being shown my future. I went through to my living room, which was all white, very big, and full of light. I saw someone sitting at a dark, wooden table, which was strange because I would never have such a heavy dark table in such a beautiful room, so I realized it was there to draw my attention.

I stared at the person sitting at the table, and even though his head was turned away, as if he didn't want to look at me, I knew it was 'L.' I called out, "What are you doing here?" He turned his head towards me, and as usual, he was very handsome. Brown eyes, brown hair and masculine. I could tell he was angry with me. I instinctively knew it was because of the spiritual show T.V. pitch. As I tuned into his thoughts, his concern became obvious. He deeply resented that I would become famous and start putting God's messages on a T.V. show or write books about my experiences. This threat bothered him tremendously.

We started arguing and I became so angry with his lack of respect for God that my eyes became icy blue and began shooting out fire. Without warning, I started to levitate towards the ceiling and my huge, white angel wings immediately appeared on my back. Crazy as it seems now, I hung perfectly still in mid-air and assumed the lotus position and started screaming at him "Do you really think you can fight me, if God, and God's power is with me?"

He immediately left, without looking back. With God's help, I had won. We had defeated 'L' again.

My Protector Screamed

It's not every time I enter the middle stage that I leave my body and go wandering off into the universes. Sometimes I experience something very different. This is one of those times.

I was living in L.A. and once again, found myself in the middle stage, very close to complete consciousness. I was aware of everything happening in my bedroom around me, but not fully awake. It is a choice I make, not to wake up totally as I'm very aware that I can travel to a different reality in which anything and everything can happen. I'm sure you can figure out why I prefer this option to waking up to the mundane reality we all live in.

However, this time was a little different. Something was lying next to me in bed, but in disguise. It wasn't just lying there, it was lying in a protective way, as if it wanted to shield me from something in the room. Then I noticed a presence lingering on my left. At first it appeared to be a light presence and I believed it was my father. Then he spoke to me in a loud voice. "Simona." In an instant the voice changed and became very dark. Immediately I knew it was 'L'. He had taken on the guise of my father. It was a classic example of how 'L' lies and cheats. He can become anything and anyone he chooses. He said to me in his dark voice. "You have worked so hard, you are dumb." As he spoke, the entity in my bed, who was my protector, screamed loudly when he heard 'L's' voice mocking me. I immediately became fully conscious and gave a silent prayer of thanks to God for his protection.

'L's' Demons -The Provocation Of The Crucifix

Previously, I have written about my experience with 'L,' but of course he has many helpers. Rebel angels, who were cast out of heaven, along with 'L' himself, the biggest rebel of them all. Even though he was God's favorite and the most beautiful archangel of all, which made archangel Michael a little envious of him, he chose to confront and defy God. Now we know that even angels and archangels have free will. 'L' defied God, so God commanded archangel Michael to expel 'L' and his rebel helpers from heaven.

The reason for 'L's' rebellion was his jealousy of God's love for his latest creation, humans. It became 'L's' mission to destroy what God loves so much; the human species. He appeals to humans' vanity and greed, by tempting them away from pursuing the greater good. Rather than using their free will for everything good, humans are now abusing their free will, much to God's dissatisfaction. This is one experience which typifies how these demons affect everyone's life, sometimes in subtle ways, sometimes very obviously.

During August 2013, I was in my apartment in Los Angeles, and I had just bought a hand sized crucifix made from wood with Jesus made from silver, and hung it above my bed, at the side I sleep on. "Oh, what provocation."

That night, I was rudely awakened as my bedroom door started banging open then closed. I heard mocking evil laughter, continuously, and knocking on the walls, even my front entrance door was opening and closing. I was so annoyed as sleep was almost impossible. That next day I put up a picture of a beautiful angel, right next to the crucifix, and said a prayer to God, "I'm asking you God that you are with me and protect me and for your gold light to always shine upon me."

I'm happy to say that the next night I wasn't disturbed and slept soundly. I guess the demons must have been given a strong message from God.

'L' Tries To Make Me Jealous

During the month of February 2018, I decided to do something about all the experiences that have been a constant part of my life since the age of fourteen. For reasons I still don't understand, I had made notes, usually handwritten, and had compiled references and a few drawings from early on, but they were not in any kind of order. The thought came that I should write a book, but I felt overwhelmed when I started looking through the material. There was so much of it, and nothing was in the least bit organized. Not only that, but the thought of reliving all those experiences was terrifying. It would be incredibly emotionally exhausting. But somewhere deep down, I knew without a doubt that I had to write the book and reveal to the world what was out there. So, with the help of a friend, the work began.

Almost immediately, I was hit with a barrage of problems, which seemed to have no end. My health deteriorated to the point where just to get out of bed in the morning was a major challenge.

Despite all this, or maybe because of it, as I knew 'L' was trying to stop me, with the help of my friend, we finally organized all the papers and began writing.

As this important phase got underway, I hoped and prayed I would not be disturbed by 'L' and one of his nightly visits. Because of my ill health, and increasing workload, I desperately needed sleep. It was not to be. On Sunday, March 11th, 2018, he made his appearance.

During the early hours on Monday, March 12th, I found myself once more in the middle stage and became aware of the all familiar feeling of the bed covers being lifted. I knew instantly that it was 'L.' As he cuddled into me, I felt his emotional longing for my soul. He held me so tight; I felt he would never let go.

In the blink of an eye, we were in another dimension, and I knew he had brought me there for a purpose. We were together in what looked like a normal room, with a wooden table and chairs. He was by the table, and walked towards me, talking to me telepathically, bragging about his adventures with other women. He stopped in front of me, and I could see he was incredibly handsome, as usual, but for some reason, he was wearing brown lipstick. Also, on his right cheek was red lipstick. He was laughing at me the whole time and mocking me, telling me how he was with other women, and tried to persuade me that I was the one that should be with him. I became so angry and appalled at his behavior that we started arguing and screaming at each other telepathically. I became so mad and frustrated that I said, "I will talk to God about your obnoxious behavior" and willed my huge, white wings to materialize right in front of him. I screamed, "I will go to God immediately."

The ceiling, which appeared solid, was in constant movement, and a space opened up. I flew straight through, noticing that I was in a huge spiral, comprised of a multitude of amazing colors, which kept on expanding. A whole different dimension was on the other side. I was in a never ending, room like space, with an enormous library stretching from wall to wall. I looked up and saw a staircase that went on forever. Suddenly, an entity appeared before me. I could tell it was female, although it defied clear definition. She stood on a second level, right above me, and I could see it wasn't a solid form. I somehow knew she was a link in my mission to see God. I asked her "Can you please take me to God? I desperately need to see Him." No sooner had I spoke that I found myself back in the room with 'L'.

We immediately started arguing again, and his words were so vile. My anger got the better of me and I screamed at him "I'm going to God, who I know loves me, and I'm going to ask his permission to destroy hell." Once again, with my angel wings spread out, I flew straight through the spiraling ceiling. Again, I found myself in the same enormous space, with the same entity waiting for me. But this time I was angry and yelled at her, "I need to see God, right now! You have to take me to him because I need his permission to destroy hell." No sooner had I said these words, I was back in bed and back in my body, fully conscious.

I felt a deep frustration because I did not see God, despite having asked twice, and pleaded with the entity. I sat in bed and pondered. The next time, I decided I would go straight to God like I normally do. I was really pissed off, angry and frustrated. I felt the entity was a coward and an idiot, and I had no doubt, the next time I would go straight to God. I don't need a middleman. I could only guess that the reason I was prevented, had something to do with 'L.' I was upset and angry the whole day.

The Creature I Followed

March- 24th, 2018, was a particularly difficult day. I wasn't feeling well and had to deal with a lot of personal problems, so I decided to go to bed early. I snuggled in, in my candle lit bedroom, with my cats beside me and appreciated the peace that descended. I soon fell asleep and I believe it must have been early morning when I was almost conscious and ready to wake up when I heard a humming sound. I'd heard the sound many times before and welcomed it. It always came when I was receiving spiritual energy. I felt my body accepting this amazing gift of energy, which I call Christ energy. My body became a state of pure ecstasy. It felt as if every cell in my body was vibrating at such a high frequency that I had no choice but to surrender to it, as it was a very powerful force. As the energy built, I felt myself levitating towards the ceiling, higher and higher.

Just as I reached this point, I found myself standing in the middle of the room looking back at my body, still in bed. This is how my numerous out of body experiences took place. However, on this occasion my astral body decided to re-enter my physical body…yes, sometimes I don't get to decide, so back in I went, and as so many other times, I felt the bed covers being lifted up, and a presence entering my bed. It was a creature unknown to me. I was at this stage, out of my body, but also still lying in my bed, consciously aware that I was in a different dimension. I looked around the room and noted it was different to my bedroom. The bed had changed, it no longer was my bed, but I was lying in this bed with the creature next to me. The creature didn't want me to see it and kept the covers over my head. It obviously didn't know that I was able to remove the covers, which of course is what I did, and took a good look at it. It was male and a mixture of man and animal. The look was far from attractive and the large amount of facial and body hair didn't help. Once the creature realized I could see him and didn't much like him, he decided to leave. I'm sure he didn't expect me to follow him, but as you all know by now, my curiosity got the better of me, and I did just that. I quickly left the bed and followed him through the door he'd just exited. I watched him walk down a long corridor and hurried to catch up. He disappeared through a door, and of course, I followed. On the other side of the door was a large room, in the middle of which, was a very wide, whitish grey, granite staircase. The creature ascended the staircase and I followed, making sure that he didn't see me.

As I reached the top, I was in another large room. I quickly scanned the room for the creature and saw him vanish down another staircase at the far end of the room. I followed him down another three staircases, so anxious to discover where he would wind up, but guess what? I ended up, back in my bed so disappointed I hadn't found out where the creature was going.

Snake Eyes

This is a very important experience for me to tell. It illustrates that the same way angels can penetrate our human dimensions, so can evil, 'L' himself, or his demons.

This experience is so unique because it happened when I was with my ex and we were both wide awake. We were lying in bed joking around and talking. It was around 11:00 at night and my ex made a joke and pulled the cover over his head while lying next to me. I followed his lead and did the same. We were face to face and looking at each other, when suddenly I saw something that to this day is still with me.

As I looked into his eyes, I saw something deeply disturbing, because the eyes looking back at me were not his eyes. They were snake eyes! They were yellow-greenish, almond shaped with a thin black slither of a pupil. I now know it was Lucifer's eyes.

The surprising thing was that my ex must have seen the same eyes as I did. He jumped out of bed and screamed, "Oh my god, oh my god." Before he said anything else, I said, "Was it the eyes?" He yelled, "Yes, I saw you had…" We both said together, "Snake eyes." He was freaking out, so I had to calm him down, and we went back to bed. He was still very uneasy, and suddenly he grabbed onto me and said in a scary voice, "Simona, Simona, there's something on my right, there's something on my right and it's really bad. I can see big black wings, they're to my right." Immediately he jumped onto me and held on tight. Again, I told him to calm down, and relax! I knew we were dealing with Lucifer. We started talking about what had just taken place, when I suddenly noticed something strange happening to the ceiling. It had split into two sections. To the left, where I was sleeping, the ceiling was white. And to the right, my ex's side, the whole ceiling had turned black. He saw it and freaked out, diving under the covers and clinging to me. You may find this hard to believe, but I wasn't scared, just annoyed, as I felt Lucifer had kind of invaded my privacy. I told my ex to stay in bed, took my crucifix, walked over to his side of the bed and told Lucifer to get the f*ck out of my bedroom, because I wasn't afraid of him and he had to leave right away. I screamed, "Get out" and stood my ground. I repeated my demands for quite a few minutes before Lucifer finally left, and eventually the room cleared up, and everything was peaceful again.

Looking back, I now realize that Lucifer's three distinctively separate appearances was directly mocking the Holy Trinity.

CHAPTER 5

Dreams

There are dreams and then there are 'Lucid' dreams. In regular dreams, you simply dream, and a lot of people don't recall dreaming when they wake up. Regular dreams can be wonderful, or they can be less so.

However, in this chapter, I will concentrate on Lucid dreams. A lot has been written about Lucid dreams, but in this case, I will explore them through my personal experiences. Since I was a child, I have always had Lucid dreams. It is of the utmost importance to understand that Lucid dreams are not the same as out of body experiences. Most of this whole book has been based on out of body experiences.

In an O.O.B.E., as has been explained throughout this book, I leave my physical body, and I am astral energy, pure soul. I have many times seen my physical body still lying in bed while knowing that I am not physical, and able to move through every dimension possible. These dimensions are only accessible by penetrating the energy membrane that separates them. A Lucid dream is a completely different phenomenon, as I will now describe with my personal experiences.

It is actually the coolest thing to have a Lucid dream because not only am I completely aware that I am dreaming, but I always make sure to tell the people in my dream, "Hey, you know we are in a dream, right?" Then I am in control of what happens in my dream, and trust me, I do everything possible to test the boundaries that I come across. I simply take control of my dreams, most of the time, by deciding who is in it, what kind of events I want to take place and the conversations I have, and with whom.

Many times, I have exercised my abilities to change the weather. I have stood in different places, looked up towards heaven, and asked for the clouds to open and send sunlight through. As soon as that happens, I will change my mind and ask for it to rain, and it does. I am in control of every single detail in most of my Lucid dreams, and can decide everything that happens and how it happens; however, there are times when I am not able to fully control the experiences. This means that I might experience knowing I am in a dream and being able to manipulate certain things within the dream, however I may not be in complete control, as the dream will unfold in a different way that I chose it to.

Dying In My Dreams

This section is unique as it is not about an out of body experience, but about dreams. Not just any dreams, but dying in my dreams, and I have had these dreams continuously over the years. Many people believe that dying in your dreams is a literal interpretation of dying in real life, but that is not the case, as you will find out later.

In my dreams, I have been stabbed to death, by various people, injected with poison and shot numbers of times.

What I want to elaborate on, is how I felt. Every time I felt myself dying it was like slowly losing consciousness, but still being aware of the people around me who had caused my death, as I was sinking into oblivion. The feeling of slowly losing consciousness, knowing I was about to die, was not as scary as I thought it might have been, but kind of a relief. In certain instances, I would be fully aware that I was dead, and surrounded by nothingness, and I remember thinking, "Wow, this is what it feels like to die," and it didn't bother me.

Next time you feel like you are dying in your dream, don't fight it, don't be afraid, let it happen. This is a way of conquering your fear. It might take many attempts to overcome your fear, but persevere, it can be done.

I am a strong believer that when you let go of your fear in your dream, and allow it to play out, resulting in your death, you will grow significantly spiritually.

It is extremely important to understand that dying in your dreams has nothing to do with dying in real life. However, in real life it is important to realize that even though the body gives in and can no longer function, the soul, which is you, continues to exist, as it is part of the ultimate source. We call that source God. The soul simply leaves the body and so do you, feeling you are still you, having a body. What happens from there on I am not able to describe since I'm still alive. However, several books on the subject, confirm that the soul is immortal.

CHAPTER 6

Experiencing Total Paralysis

Most people would find this next experience totally horrifying, but for some reason, I found it extremely peaceful and relaxing.

Once again, I found myself in the middle stage, but this time it was different. My body was completely and utterly paralyzed.

I was consciously aware that I could not move any part of my physical body at all. I had never experienced this sensation before. As I was dwelling over this and realizing how different it felt, I suddenly was aware of the Christ energy entering my being, making every cell in my body vibrate. This energy is so utterly amazing that I am constantly longing for it and recently prayed to God, asking to receive it, as the feeling is so incredible. Not only did I get the energy, but it came four times in succession.

As I was lying there, I looked towards my bedroom door and realized that the door was opened inwards, which is impossible, as the hinges can't work that way, and I immediately knew I was in another dimension. I decided to get up and close the door, meaning my astral body left my physical body, which could not move, and closed the door. I had no idea why I was stupid enough to go back into my body, but in I went, only to find out that my physical body was still paralyzed.

Being back in my body I was thinking to myself, "I bet the stupid door has opened again in the wrong direction." I looked towards the door and guess what? That's exactly what had happened.

At this point, I was so irritated at my body being completely paralyzed that I decided to put up a fight just to see if I could win.

I started fighting the paralyses, only to find out it was almost impossible. I used every ounce of will power, and thought processes I could find, to shake off the paralyses. Never had I thought this hard for so long in order to overcome a spiritual challenge.

After an incredible mental struggle, I finally managed to regain full consciousness and was able to wake up and move my body.

Then I thought, why did I do that? I have such a curious nature, I wished I had decided differently, therefore I made a promise to myself that next time, which I am totally looking forward to, I would allow myself to remain paralyzed, without fighting, just to see where this will take me.

I hope that what I will experience will be what so many other people have described. Extra-terrestrial encounters! Considering that I have already had so many of these and all extremely interesting and positive, I will await more.

CHAPTER 7

Ulla And Darlene

I have a very evolved mentor whose name is Ulla Runchel. Not only is she a spiritual mentor, but also an author and songwriter.

She used to reside in Spain, but now she lives in Denmark. Ulla and I met under the most unusual circumstances. Five or six years ago, my mother decided (without telling me) to bring Ulla with her when she came to visit me in Los Angeles. Both my mother and Ulla thought it was a great idea, just to show up without telling me.

It was the first time Ulla and I had met, and the first request I made to her was "Can you please give me a healing?" She told me to go to my bedroom and close my eyes. I started feeling a warmth spreading through my body. I couldn't help but take a peek, and saw Ulla holding both hands about a foot above my body. Shortly after, I felt every molecule in my body had been energized, and was tingling and vibrating, and I felt as if my body was lifting off

the bed. The sensation was indescribable. She then took her finger and gently poked me in my armpit, wrist and other places on my body. The feeling was amazing. The best way I can describe it is, it was as if my whole body became like electricity. When the healing was finished, I felt extremely calm, relaxed and at peace.

Through the years, Ulla, as my mentor has helped me profoundly. Not only has she sent me many power healings, which wipes me out for a whole day, as my system regenerates, but also has her own way of taking my inner anxiety and fear away so I can't feel it. Ulla is what I consider to be one of the most evolved, selfless, humble and incredible beings on this planet earth.

Darlene

I have a very dear friend, her name is Darlene King, also known as the Barrington medium, based on the east coast and is a world renowned psychic medium and intuitive healer. Darlene and I have been friends for quite a while and around two years ago we set up a skype session to discuss a possible project.

As we were in the middle of our conversation, Darlene suddenly stopped talking and looked at me, her eyes wide open, tears streaming down her face. She said, "Simona, oh my God, I just saw something happen, something behind you."

At that very moment, after she had spoken those words, I felt a complete change in my body and in my mind. Suddenly, I sat up straighter. A calm entered my body and mind. I felt my eyes change and became focused in a totally different way, and most of all as I spoke, my voice changed completely. It was calmer, and deeper than my normal voice, and very controlled, as if someone was talking through me. I asked Darlene "What did you see, Darlene?" Her answer was a revelation to me. "Simona, I just saw a huge white light being, could have been an angel, and that light entered your body, and you completely changed." I said, "Darlene, I can feel I have changed. I feel fantastic."

I have relayed this story because I understand how important it is to be factual. I spent five years in law school and one of the first things you learn is that witnesses are very important if your story is to be believed.

CHAPTER 8

Do Animals Go To Heaven?

This chapter will be different, as it is very near and dear to my heart, and I hope answers many of the questions that concern a lot of people. "Do animals go to heaven?"

I have always been attracted to animals because of their innocence and purity, in fact, animals are the most innocent creatures that walk the earth. There is nothing I love more than animals.

I've always had animals as part of my life. Horses, dogs and especially cats, and one cat, Pumpkin, was the love of my life. I loved this innocent creature beyond anything I have ever loved. He was a white, Persian Chinchilla, with big green eyes and huge paws. We were inseparable. He would sleep next to me every night, and always have his paw on my hand.

After thirteen years it was his time to pass and I was inconsolable. I was both in emotional and physical pain for almost three years. I remember crying every single night for a whole year. I had great problems accepting his passing. I used to wake up every other night in the middle stage, yelling out to God, "Can you hear me? God, do you hear me? Show me. Give me a sign that you hear me. Please send me my beloved beautiful cat."

One night, God answered me. I was in the middle stage, when I saw the ceiling dissolving. My duvet fell over my face and was gently held there, preventing me from seeing. I couldn't accept that, as I needed to see. However, before I could remove the cover, I felt movement on the duvet. I could feel paws walking on me, towards my face. I was ecstatic. I knew it was my beautiful white, pure wonderful baby cat, Pumpkin, my ultimate loved one. He had come to comfort me. He knew how much I missed and loved him, more than anything in the world.

I am aware that God allowed him to come from heaven to comfort me because I asked God to please grant me this wish. I managed to move the cover away from my face, and there he was! I saw his white, adorable face, and beautiful soft, loving eyes, looking at me with peace and love.

I am the one who suffered, not him. He is in God's heaven. I caressed him, held him and kissed him, and I am eternally grateful for the little time I spent with him. Since then, he has been allowed to visit me many times over a period of years. Heaven is for both humans and animals.

CHAPTER 9

Do Angels Really Exist?

"Do Angels really exist?" is a question that has been asked over and over, going way back. I can categorically say that in my experience they most certainly do. This chapter will describe my personal experience seeing angels. A lot of them were witnessed by other people, and almost all of them occurred when I was fully awake.

I woke up between 5 a.m. and 6 a.m. which I do on a regular basis, and now realize that it may not be coincidental, as it happens to be the time I was born. To be more precise, I was in Los Angeles at the time, and my actual birth time in Denmark was 2:00 p.m. There is a nine hour time difference.

As I woke up, I saw like so many times before, a small angel fly past my face, no more than inches away. I followed it with my eyes as it flew right to left. The feathery wings were beating very quickly. Then immediately after, I saw a human size angel, flying very slowly by, barely moving its wings. It lingered for a while over my bed so I could take a close look at it. This was by far the most unusual angel I had ever seen. The incredible thing was that half the angel was white, and half was darker. One wing was white, the other darker. Even though one half was darker, it was positive. The angel had many symbols all over it, that I had never seen before.

After it had lingered for a little while, it disappeared. My attention was drawn to my T.V. in the corner of the room. Above the T.V. was a brilliant diamond that exploded into a white flash of beautiful light.

Angels Wake Me Up

I woke up in my bedroom at the usual time, between 5 a.m. and 6 a.m., opened my eyes, and thought, "This is crazy, I don't want to be awake this early, it's halfway through the night. It's really annoying."

Right in front of my face, no more than four inches away was a pair of hand sized white wings beating rapidly, moving slowly past me. Then I noticed just three inches below was another set of wings, white and sleek, but barely moving, even though the angel was going past me. I saw everything crystal clear, it was very real, and I eventually went back to sleep.

This continues to happen, even to this day.

Angel Cherubs Revealing Their Presence

Sometime during my marriage, we were in our apartment. It was evening and we had lit a lot of candles. I noticed that the room began to fill with all kinds of white light. There was a continuous movement of energy, and the room then filled with silver glitter. I, of course, saw all of this, but continued the conversation with my ex. However, he noticed my gaze was moving around the room, and he followed it and froze. He blurted out, "There's something here." He went quiet and focused, "Oh my God, I see small Cherubs."

By this time, the room was full of tiny angels, so small in fact that they could sit on your hand. They had wings that were full of glitter and randomly flew around. My ex now totally enchanted, walked towards them and said, "Simona, do you see?" I nodded and got up and walked over. We both reached out to touch them, and they sat on our hands, but we couldn't feel them.

After this experience, we continued seeing Angels and cherubs together, on many occasions.

My Girlfriend And I Witnessed Angels

My girlfriend and I were in my apartment. It was early evening and we were hanging out. We didn't have candles, but the central chandelier was lit. Suddenly, we both noticed a lot of movement coming from the space around the light. We walked over and watched in amazement as small and big cherubs started taking shape. The large ones had white, feathery wings and the small ones had glitter wings. We were ecstatic. We reached out our hands and were amazed to be able to touch them, even though we couldn't feel them and even more surprised when they sat on our hands. It was a truly awesome experience.

GOD Sent Me An Angel

I was in Los Angeles, asleep, and needed to wake up to use the bathroom. I checked the time, and surprise, surprise, it was 5:00 a.m. Before I was able to get my butt out of bed, I saw very clearly a human like body, with large, translucent wings coming through the far wall. It floated from the wall right next to me and lingered for a couple of seconds, before disappearing through the wall behind me. Then the urge to use the bathroom overcame me and I bolted out of bed.

The Cherub I Kissed

One of the most precious memories I've had with angels occurred when I was at home in Los Angeles. I was sitting up in bed, fully awake, as it was early evening. I looked towards the mirror on the wall and to my surprise I saw a beautiful cherub, bigger than the usual ones I was familiar with, flying towards me. It had wings that were white and feathery and it's face was like a real baby, quite beautiful, and childish with a sweetness that was breathtaking. It flew straight towards me, and as I sat up and leaned forward, just as it reached me, I kissed it on its little mouth, and then it was gone.

My Ex Saw Angels In My Bedroom

I was home in Los Angeles, taking a nap during the day, which I normally don't do, and my then husband was at work.

I woke up early afternoon and exited my bedroom, feeling very peaceful. I entered the living room and to my surprise found my husband sitting on the couch, completely still, with his hands in his lap. I asked him what he was doing.

He looked at me in a weird way and described to me what he had just witnessed. He had come home early, during my nap, and opened the bedroom door. He had seen the whole room lit up with a bluish light. I was lying on the bed asleep and covered with all kinds and sizes of white beautiful angels. They covered my body, and occupied all the space in the room.

He told me he had looked at the scene in absolute awe and then gently closed the bedroom door, before returning to the living room couch.

Visiting Angel Heaven

In one of my many out of body experiences, I visited angel heaven. As I was already an astral body, and in another dimension, I found myself flying into a grand space, inside of which was another space. A long opening appeared before me and I flew through and abruptly stopped, mesmerized by what I saw. I was in a space filled with soft, warm, white light, and a feeling of utter peace and stillness overwhelmed me. Everything was bliss. Everywhere I looked, I saw countless angels, humanlike with large, white, feathery wings. When I got over my astonishment, I realized I also had my white feather archangel wings on my back.

I instinctively knew without doubt, that I belonged there. This was my true home.

I discovered that part of my job as an angel was to pick up souls from earth, that were destined for heaven. I remember picking up a very fat man, and thought "How can I possibly carry that overweight person?" But with no effort whatsoever, I picked him up and flew to heaven.

The Angel Who Tried To Deceive Me

As I was lying in my bed, in the middle stage, an angel flew into my bedroom and landed on my bed. It was a big angel, sitting there looking at me. I asked, "Are you God's angel?" It hugged me with its wings, but I felt something was wrong, and I asked it again, "Are you God's angel?" It didn't answer. I took a closer look at it and noticed that it had wings that were withered and ugly. I pushed it away and it laughed, showing long discolored fangs for teeth.

I became furious and looked it straight in the eyes and asked, "Do you see any fear? Get the f**k out of here, I'm much stronger than you!" I said this with confidence, knowing that I had archangel Gabriel's powers and God's help. I felt and showed no fear, and because of my strength, the deceiving angel became frightened and left.

I looked up towards the ceiling, and it dissolved, showing another dimension which looked like God's heaven. I asked God to send me a real angel, and he did, right away. Another beautiful, fair angel flew towards me. It had big gold wings. It sat in front of me and hugged me. It was beautiful and I felt at total peace.

CHAPTER 10

Near-Near Death Experience

Some people have heard of near- death experiences, and an increasing number have had both near- death and near-near- death personal experience, which often changes their lives forever. As you may have guessed already, I did have my own experiences. The first one occurred while I was in L.A.

I agreed reluctantly to go for dinner at my girlfriend's house, to meet her father, whom I had never met. I knew it meant a lot to her, as she considered me to be one of her best friends. My dilemma was that I had already made plans to go to dinner with my best friend the same night, so I had to contact him and cancel, rather than disappoint my girlfriend who depended on me being there. Both friends meant a lot to me, so the thought of having to pick up the phone and cancel on a friend really stressed me out.

I picked up the phone, around early afternoon and called my dear friend, I explained to him that my girlfriend wanted me to meet her father, and as it was so important to her, I agreed. My friend's reaction took me by surprise. He wouldn't accept my decision. He kept on pushing me to cancel with my girlfriend which was extremely stressful for me. I then called my girlfriend and told her I might not be able to attend dinner with her father. I could not believe how angry she became, insisting that I had to show up. I then called back my other friend, to explain my dilemma. My girlfriend's father was elderly, and it was the only opportunity we had to meet, so I really had no choice. Once again, he reacted in a totally unsympathetic way, insisting that I kept our arrangement.

By this time, I had spent an hour with back and forth phone calls. To complicate my situation, I had two other girlfriends visiting and I was trying to figure out how to keep everyone happy. My two girlfriends were hanging out in my bedroom while I was having these stressful phone conversations in the guest bedroom. As the stress levels built, I became more and more anxious, verging on panic, when suddenly something happened in my brain. I was sitting on my bed when I felt a click in the back of my head.

Without warning, I suddenly lost all my sight. Everything went black. I started screaming! I realized I had just gone blind. I stumbled off the bed, feeling utter panic and helplessness. I staggered through to my bedroom, banging into walls and furniture, screaming and crying. "I'm blind," I cried. "Help me." To my astonishment, both my girlfriends started laughing calling me an actress and a great drama queen.

I couldn't understand their reactions. They didn't believe me, so I stood still and yelled, "I'm blind, I can't see. Something just clicked in my brain. You've got to get me to a hospital." One of my girlfriends finally saw that I was not joking, it was for real, and took my hand and led me down to the garage. We got into my car and she drove me to the local emergency room. I was checked in immediately. I was placed in a room and a top neurologist hurried in to check me out. At this time, a small portion of my sight had returned. They did a series of tests on me including a spinal tap. For those of you that have not had experience with this, trust me, don't do it. It is the most painful experience ever. I spent that night in the hospital and by morning, my sight had gradually returned to almost normal.

The neurologist returned and informed me that I'd had a stroke due to prolonged, high levels of stress and prescribed drugs which I had to take twice daily. I took the medicine for a couple of days and to my horror, my sight deteriorated, in a very specific way. It was like a curtain, closing the world out. After five days, I could only see a small portion of the world, directly in front of me. A strong feeling, from deep in my soul, told me I had to stop taking the pills, so I threw them out. Within a couple of days my sight gradually began to return.

During the darkest time of this episode, right before I ditched the pills, I was in a very bad place, and truly thought I was about to die. I was sinking into a black hole, with no way out. The same night that I decided to ditch the pills, and my sight began to open, I was lying in bed when suddenly a host of light beings surrounded my bed, up to my chest. The fact that I could see these incredible light beings was God's way of confirming my decision to throw away the pills. He was protecting me.

The light beings were human in shape, medium height, and appeared to be made of white marble, although with a translucent quality. Their features were indistinguishable, apart from one. The nearest being less than two feet away, was a slim female, with long dark hair, slender arms and hands, and exuded pure love. She took a step towards me and stretched out her arms, trying to touch me. It took me by surprise, and I jumped back a little. I wish to this day that I had not reacted, and let her touch me, because now I know it was Holy Mary.

I am happy to say that my sight almost fully returned, and I believe that God sent Holy Mary to help me through the difficult ordeal.

I believe Holy Mary was sent to pull me up from the hole of deep despair I was in when I sincerely thought I was going to die, as I was almost completely blind.

However, there was an incredible follow up to this experience. After my stroke, I was given the diagnosis which said the cerebral artery which provides most of the blood to the brain had burnt out, causing the stroke, and the doctors prognosis was that it was irreparable. If it wasn't for all the small arteries, which contained the blood supply, I would have been dead

Extra Terrestrial-Intervention

During the night of Oct 15th and 16th, I was in Los Angeles, when something extraordinary happened. I was lying in bed when I started to receive a divine energy. My whole body was vibrating, and I was transported immediately into the middle stage, but ninety nine percent conscious. I was completely aware of everything that was happening. I levitated halfway between my bed and the ceiling. I felt a pair of hands firmly holding my head steady. I heard a very calm female voice with pleasant authority. She was talking to other beings that were surrounding me. I was unable to see or speak to these beings, but will can move mountains, so with all my strength, I managed to pose one question. I asked the female entity "What are you doing to my brain?" as I had a strong feeling that was her purpose. I knew she was surprised to hear me speak. She hesitated but then answered, "Oh, just giving you something to relax the muscles." I knew, or rather felt she wasn't telling me the truth. I knew she had inserted a needle into my brain, but I didn't feel it. I then clearly felt a cold liquid flowing into my brain. It was a pleasant and calm sensation which didn't hurt. Strangely enough the whole thing didn't seem to bother me too much, but I was curious about what exactly they had injected into my brain.

Suddenly I was able to see, and all around me was white and flashing. Also, to my amazement, I saw a human figure, a well-dressed man, wearing a business suit, who appeared to be overseeing the procedure. The thought crossed my mind, why had they adopted the disguise, as I knew they were extra-terrestrial beings. I can only assume it was to alleviate any fear, to make me more comfortable.

The Discovery

In 2006, I decided to revisit the hospital that did my initial MRI/MRA and have my brain checked as I was unsure how much stress my body and especially my brain would take, as the doctors had told me that only the smaller brain arteries were supporting my physical system, and the fact that I was a gym freak concerned me.

I entered the MRI room and lay down while the machine clanked away, taking a record of what was happening inside my skull. I was fearful of the result as I didn't want any further bad news. It was one thing to know the blood supply to my brain had been severely compromised, but it would be much worse to find out my situation had deteriorated.

Half an hour later, I sat in the doctor's office, my fear increasing, waiting for the results. The doctor entered holding a file, with a puzzled look on her face. "It's good news," she said. "We are not entirely sure how, but your main artery has completely recovered and healed. It's working perfectly normal, as if nothing had happened."

I looked at her, part in relief, mostly in surprise and said, "How is this possible?" She answered, "Sometimes the body can heal itself, but this is a miracle."

I have had countless encounters with extra-terrestrials, almost all of them written down and recorded. Every encounter has been amazing. Not once have I felt fear.

Jesus Heals

I was living in Los Angeles and my mother was visiting, when out of the blue, a violent fever hit me, as I was shopping at a supermarket. Suddenly, my temperature skyrocketed to 103.6 and I started to shiver uncontrollably. My mother managed to get me home and insisted I go to the hospital.

As I was lying in bed, shivering, listening to my mother in the other room trying to persuade me to get to the hospital, I looked up and to my astonishment, on my left side, standing next to me, I saw Jesus. He was wearing a white robe, had shoulder length long, brownish hair, very compassionate eyes, and looked exactly like the many pictures of him.

He looked into my eyes with absolute love, and compassion, but also a decisiveness. He placed his hand on my solar plexus and I felt an extreme heat, like a hot iron, but it didn't burn me. While this was happening, my mother, next door, packing things to take me to the E.R. was still screaming at me. "We need to go to the emergency room now!" I yelled back, as loud as I could, "No, Mom, I don't need to, Jesus is here and he's healing me right now." A short while later, Jesus disappeared, and my fever totally vanished.

Two weeks later, the exact same thing happened. I was lying in bed shaking with a cold, and a fever of 103.6, and Jesus appeared. Once again, he placed his hand on my solar plexus and I felt indescribable heat but did not burn. I recovered immediately.

CHAPTER 11

Jesus, Holy Mary And Levitation

In 2016, I was in Los Angeles, and my longing to leave my body and experience the freedom of being in different dimensions continued to dominate a lot of my time, as I got an enormous kick out of being free of gravity.

One night, as I was in the middle stage, I looked up, and standing right next to my bed was Jesus. He must have felt my uncontrollable desire to leave my body because he reached out his hand and I took it. He pulled me out. I was free and ecstatic.

The extraordinary thing was, that I could see I was in two places at the same time. I was in my bed and at the same time lying on a sunbed in another dimension having a conversation with my brother. I know this sounds impossible. How can anyone be in two different places at the same time? So, I checked. I returned to my bed, fully aware that I was also, still talking to my brother. I know

Jesus came to me specifically on this occasion, to show me that it was possible to be in two places at the same time; to bi-locate.

Holy Mary Helping Me Levitate

My next experience was very interesting. Not just because of the three separate occasions I was able to levitate, but also because of the continuing actions of the next day.

Early in the morning of Thursday the 19th, November 2009, I was suddenly overcome by the intense divine energy that I had experienced many times previously and that I always long for. Again, my whole body was in ecstasy. I felt every cell in my body vibrating with an intensity that was indescribable. I immediately levitated towards the ceiling and as I looked down towards the bed, I saw lots of slender hands lifting my astral body. The hands were beautiful, long and marble like in appearance. Suddenly, I was back in my physical body, and for the second time, I again received the divine energy. I totally allowed my body to surrender to this divine ecstatic energy. Once again, I levitated towards the ceiling and witnessed the same hands carrying my astral body. Once more I finished up in my physical body.

I made the conscious decision, if I received the energy a third time, I would completely surrender and allow my body to levitate through the ceiling, as I realized this was an energy membrane that I needed to penetrate, in order to access another dimension.

Sure enough, I received the energy a third time and levitated through the ceiling, but only for a second, before I was back in my body much too soon, which was disappointing because what I was longing for was to escape my physical body and become one with everything.

What happened next was in the real world. I awoke the next morning and decided to attend church. As I entered, I decided to sit in the first row. After a while, Veronica, one of the church congregation I knew, came to sit beside me. We talked for a while, and she mentioned (as she had done many times before) to remember to pay attention to the Holy Mother of God, the Virgin Mary.

Suddenly, I had a revelation, that when I had previously lit a candle at church, I realized I had prayed in a very specific way that was unusual. "I dedicate this candle to anyone in Heaven who wishes to help me." I had not named anyone in my prayer, but had allowed whoever wished to help me, to do so. It then became very clear to me that it was Virgin Mary.

She was there for me when I had a stroke, standing by my bed and stretching out her hands to touch me, and it was her that helped me levitate by carrying my astral body. I recognized the beautiful marble hands. I decided to light some candles for my animals that had passed, but the lighter didn't work as it was out of gas. I tried again, no luck, so I said a prayer "I'm lighting this candle for the divinity in heaven who is helping me, that I now know is you, Holy Mary." Again, I clicked the lighter, even though it was out of gas, but to my amazement it lit with a huge flame, which I saw as being an incredible sign.

Holy Mary

This next experience took me by complete surprise. I was visited by Holy Mary, which I found unusual, because until recently I had not paid much attention to her.

It happened on February 27th, 2018. On this occasion, I was asleep, and I had an incredibly vivid dream. This was not an out of body experience, but a dream. I saw Holy Mary's face, up to five different times during the night, each time separately, she kept coming back.

She appeared to me, just as I'd seen her in many pictures, and with a most wonderful, loving, compassionate smile. Covering her head was a beautiful blue scarf. All around her head were bright white and gold glitter lights. These visions kept on appearing all night, or so it felt, and I felt deeply that the reason for Holy Mary's visit was a sign of approval, because we had started the process of writing God's book, and I could tell she was pleased because we were doing God's work.

CHAPTER 12

The Power Of Forgiveness

Two thousand years ago, Jesus taught us about betrayal and forgiveness. His message from the cross was, "Forgive them father, for they know not what they do."

By following Jesus's teaching, I was able to forgive what to me at the time felt like a betrayal.

I cannot write this without mentioning God's son, Jesus, who was here on this earth to teach us about forgiveness. He was capable of complete forgiveness, as he was the son of God, meaning God lives within him, through his soul, which filled him completely. Forgiveness is one of the hardest things for humans to learn. Not only must we forgive ourselves, which I have a hard time doing, but we must learn to forgive others, which doesn't mean we have to forget, but we must learn to forgive, and it has to come from a pure place, it has to come from the soul.

In order to portray what it means to forgive I have decided to reveal a personal experience. I made the decision to do this in order to demonstrate that if I could forgive, so can you.

During one of my out of body experiences, as my physical body lay in bed, my astral body was walking around my bedroom, and ended up in front of my large mirror. As I looked at myself, I saw two huge archangel wings pop out of my back. I looked at the wings in amazement. They were so grand and beautiful. As I gazed around, I saw the most incredible colors. Lavender blue, purple and white lights, sparkling in the air. I was completely aware that I was having an O.O.B.E., as the lights merged with my face, and I became one with the energy.

As I focused on my wings in the mirror, they unfolded and closed without any apparent effort on my part. I was absolutely dumbfounded, speechless, happy beyond belief.

I suddenly realized I was not alone in the room. I looked in the mirror again and was so surprised to see that someone was sitting on the bed behind me.

Then something unusual happened. Without warning, my wings flipped backwards and slapped the person in the face, before returning to their normal position.

That should have told me something, but I chose to ignore it.

One night, my ex and I came back from an evening out and he told me to sit down as he had something important to tell me.

He was very intoxicated as he said, "What I'm about to tell you now will change everything." He continued by telling me that he hadn't been happy in our relationship for a while. He hated being in the city. He was a country boy at heart and longed to go back to nature.

I asked him, "How long have you felt this way? Has it been for more than a year?" He said, "Yes, it has" and then went totally silent.

I refused to believe it. I simply couldn't understand what he was telling me. I just sat there, totally still, trying to figure out what had just happened. To say I was in shock was an understatement. I felt he had betrayed my trust by not confiding in me a lot earlier.

One thing I realized was that once the shock had settled, the pain would take over. The only slightly consoling thing about the whole mess, was that he had the courage to tell me to my face, and not just leave the relationship. He then said that he understood that I would find it difficult if not impossible to forgive him.

However, I was surprised to discover that I was able to forgive him. As I spoke the words, "I forgive you," I knew that I meant every word. I felt it from deep within my soul. I was completely capable of forgiving him.

I knew, even as I spoke, it was only a matter of time before the pain would set in. During this conversation, we had been sitting on the floor, but I rose and moved to sit on the couch, and purposefully turned my back to him, as he remained sitting on the floor. I then started to pray silently to God. "God, whatever happens from here on out, I have truly and completely forgiven him. You just must do me one favor. Please never ever let me feel the pain." I strongly begged for this to happen, and as I was praying, I was aware that something unusual was taking place. I felt an angelic force entering my body and merging with my soul. I noticed my posture straightening, and a calmness came over me.

God had granted me his gift of never feeling the pain, because I had been completely capable of forgiving from the depths of my soul.

Later, as I thought through what had just occurred, I understood that God's son Jesus, had taught this very lesson 2000 years ago. How to forgive from the soul, and I thought, if Jesus could forgive all of humanity, for it's horrendous behavior, then I could forgive this human flaw. I should, of course, and learn from Jesus that this was the right choice.

I feel this is the lesson for many people; if I can forgive the betrayal I felt, you can forgive too. Whatever has happened to you, whoever has done you harm or wrong, it is important to learn forgiveness, that way you will be set free of pain. Maybe not immediately, but it will happen. As soon as you do this, you release yourself from other people's control over your thoughts, emotions, and actions. Forgiving is simply evolving and learning from God's son.

CHAPTER 13

The Van

During May 2018, I had a very significant and vivid dream.

I was in a van sitting in the very back seat, to the right. I had no idea who was driving the van. As I looked out of the window, I realized that the van was hurtling down the highway at an incredible speed, way beyond any vehicle's capability. As a matter of fact, it felt like I was in a 'min' jet, we were traveling so fast. Then, incredibly the speed increased further. I began to feel nervous. I tried to see who was driving but couldn't because I was so far back. I looked out of the front window and saw another car emerge from a side street, directly in front of the van, and I thought, "Oh my God, we're gonna crash," but somehow the van maneuvered around the car and continued going. The van was moving so fast that soon it was tailgating another vehicle. I thought "sh*t! Were definitely gonna hit this one." To the driver's credit, he somehow managed to get out of the way, escaping by mere inches. The van continued to drive, faster than I can possibly describe. At this point, I really needed to know who was driving. I started crawling towards the front seat, and when I reached the seat behind the driver's seat, I realized to my amazement that there was no driver. My instinct told me to quickly grab the wheel to control the van, in order to avoid any kind of accident.

Then the most peculiar thing happened. For the first time in my life, I let go of control. I instinctively knew I had to sit back and let the van drive itself.

When I woke up, I realized I had just been through a test. I had been given the choice of trying to control every aspect of my life, including writing this book, or to simply allow God to take control. This was probably one of the biggest lessons in letting go of control and having complete faith in God.

I believe everyone should pay attention to the words spoken by so many, "Let go, let God." If a person can do that, they will become one with the flow, and things will turn out the way they should turn out. I can tell you from my own personal experience, that by deciding to be in the flow, by allowing God to be in control, my life has changed profoundly.

CHAPTER 14

Meeting GOD

This chapter has been one of the most difficult to write because it touched upon subjects that I don't feel qualified to write about. It goes into such detail about God, Archangel Gabriel, and my small part in the great plan, that I know it is way beyond my comprehension. It would have been easier to write a watered-down version of this message, but then I would not be doing God's work, so I have tried to relate everything I was told verbatim. The message came to me during the daytime, and I was fully awake. The thoughts came so fast that I had to speed write.

My experience of channeling is that when I am channeled through it happens unexpectedly. Suddenly, my brain is filled with information so profound that I know beyond doubt they are not my own thoughts. This information comes from a much higher power, and my job, in this case, is to quickly find a pen and paper and start writing.

Sometimes, I have managed to write fifteen to twenty pages. My ex would witness this phenomenon and was astounded how much I would write in such a short period of time.

I feel I have to make it clear that in no way did I ever imagine I could be part of anything as significant as the messages I received, or indeed any of the events described in this book, and feel so humble to be able to pass on the information, which I repeat, does not come from me. I am simply the messenger.

The Message

This is God channeling through me: "Therefore you now are the chosen one, chosen by me-the ultimate light, and by him, the ultimate darkness. In this covenant you represent the key. The key to either keep heaven open for all human souls, for eternity, or to lock the door to paradise forever, so no light will shine, and darkness will rule forever. The outcome depends on your actions as the chosen one. The key lives within your heart. If you can keep faith and not succumb to human greed and selfishness, and thereby doubt my existence, you will succeed in your mission"

As the message continued, I realized I was being told what God had already planned with archangel Gabriel, the only archangel, that I'm aware of, that consists of female energy, contrary to all of God's other archangels, which are male energy.

Message Continues

"In order to make earth the playground for this test, it must be a test on equal terms between good and evil. Therefore, I will now erase your memory, then you will become part of a human soul which has already been chosen. This human was chosen because of her weakness and confusion as she did not believe in me, as a person of faith would, having already been seduced by the dark, and thereby almost lost faith in me. I leave you to take that last grain of hope that still occupies a small piece of her soul and turn that into an ultimate awareness, and belief in my existence, so that she will make a conscious choice forever worshipping my light, and forever turn her back upon the dark one."

Message Continues

"Simona, you are an important part of the puzzle, and to save human- kind by preventing them from self-destruction, you must give messages of hope. That is why I have showed to you the ultimate truth, by taking you to my kingdom, but also let you see that dark wants to conquer.

My Explanation

I need to make it very clear that I do not walk around on this planet earth thinking I'm an angel with angel wings. Unfortunately, I feel very human. However, when I'm able to access other dimensions, I am granted the privilege of wearing Gabriel's big beautiful archangel wings. That's when I can feel her the most. In these other dimensions, however, I am also able to take on a different persona. For example, when I accessed the devil's den, it was as a little boy, and I can't count the many times when I have seen myself as someone else entirely, with different hair color, etc. It is important to know that when you access other dimensions and become someone else, it usually is chosen for you.

GOD Continues To Enlighten Me.

To find the perfect way to introduce God was difficult, but I think if I explain the following, everything will make perfect sense.

Before I met God, he began channeling to me, most times with messages I didn't understand until much later, and sometimes, not even now, so I will relate my first message, just as I received it.

One day, as I was in my apartment, I was bombarded with messages that were so profound, and way outside my usual frame of reference. I realized they were messages that were very special and grabbed a pen and paper and began writing. My pen literally flew over the paper, the results of which are as follows.

"God, you are truly perfect, the creator of everything and challenger of nothing/emptiness. Only you know the answer to all our questions and to what truly lies behind the aspect and meaning of creation. Most of us wish to see you, to speak to you and to truly feel you, in all your greatness; then again, only a few get to come close to you, as only you choose who will see and feel you. Only some of us are chosen and that is for a reason."

When I read the messages, I was astounded, and somewhat shaken and had no idea what I had written. I pondered for days on the meanings, but came to no conclusions, until later, a second message was channeled. Again, I write it as it came to me, unaware of any of the content until I read it later. I make no claim to the subject of the message, even though I am mentioned by name, and ask that you don't judge my honesty in recounting every word verbatim.

"So, Simona, when you are the one to be trusted to participate in the most grand secret of the universe, and your world's in it, as it is to you, or is it? Then you must know how to prepare. Seek more knowledge, but only from the right sources. Read what I wrote-it must go to you, you will understand. By now you realize that you play a significant part in the major puzzle. You do see, and you will see what I created and that is for a reason. Now you are impatient, little one, but you will see, and you must be ready to see, and you will soon. So, you were the 'lucky one' to be chosen. Now you must be strong. She is a part of you, and you are part of her, as two pieces of a puzzle that can't be separated and must rely on each other in order to conquer."

I am now aware that when He refers to what He created it means the multitude of different dimensions I have now traveled to.

The only way I could visit these dimensions was by having pure astral energy.

The reference to "She becomes part of me" will be covered later in the battle for heaven.

GOD Sends Me a Sign

This experience is a little strange because two days prior, I knew I had to go to mass at my local church. I don't know how I knew. I just knew.

So, on Saturday, August 10th, 2013, I attended mass. I was late, and I don't remember why, but as I entered church, I felt the Holy Spirit consuming my whole being and started crying.

I sat in church and followed the mass, and began praying, and pondered the mystery of faith. I realized it was no mystery to me because I had seen and therefore, I believe. To me it was a fact.

After mass, as I was sitting praying a woman of a certain age came over to me and sat down, looked me in the eyes and said "God loves you. He hears your prayers." She went on to say, "I couldn't pray because I kept on getting this message." She said, "This has never happened to me before, but God was so insistent I talk to you and pass on the message." Again, she gazed at me with tears in her eyes. Then she made an unusual remark, looking at my jacket she said, "It says angel on you."

I knew I had received a major important sign from God, most likely due to the incident that happened the previous night in my bedroom. I had to confront "L" twice as he came towards me in my bedroom. I told him yet again, that I was not afraid of him and to get out of my bedroom right away. I called for God, but God did not show up. Realizing I was in another dimension, I strongly willed for my wings to come out, but they didn't. This was highly unusual, as I always get my wings in any other dimension. I kept on calling upon God. "Don't ever abandon me again. I know I am entrusted."

As I sat in church, having just received the message from a stranger, and recalling the previous night's events, I said out loud, "My belief in, and love for your son is completely filling me, and also my love for you God."

Meeting GOD For The First Time

My first meeting with God was the most incredible experience imaginable. I was in L.A., living in an apartment in West Hollywood. It was early in the morning and I remember distinctly it was May 2004.

I was in bed, in the middle stage, unwilling to wake up when suddenly I was transported to another dimension without going through an O.O.B.E. I was in a large, open space that felt like an apartment. I was in a temporary holding area, deciding which way to go. It was all about me having to choose. As I was waiting, 'L' showed up. I knew immediately it was him. He had taken on the persona of an attractive, dark-haired man, doing everything in his power to tempt me. He talked to me in a quiet voice, asking me to go with him, but I declined. For some reason, I knew there was something amazing waiting for me. 'L' had to leave at that point, as there were rules, which he had to obey.

No sooner had he departed than Archangel Michael showed up. There was no doubt in my mind it was him as we had met several times before.

Archangel Michael appeared to me as a blond, young man. Extremely handsome, with a chiseled face, blue eyes, and enormous white wings on his back. He was almost seven feet tall, with a translucent appearance.

I knew he was there to comfort and help me as he looked at me in a very loving way. Suddenly the room began to turn slowly and from the center, a large round marble podium rose from the floor, which was also turning. I watched in amazement as a throne appeared on the podium. There was a white marble figure sitting there and I knew without a shadow of a doubt that it was God.

I was drawn to Him and started walking towards Him. I stopped in front of him and looked into his eyes. He had taken on the presence of a very ancient old man made from the whitest marble I had ever seen. He sat in peace and looked into my eyes. There are no words to describe how His eyes looked, they were beyond any comprehension, but I will try my best. They were a brown that I've never seen before. As I stood there in wonder, looking into the incredible eyes, I was aware of a total understanding and love, but also pain for the human species, and a complete knowledge of all things.

As He was looking at me, He took my hand in His, and held it tight. He reached out and placed two white marble fingers on my arm. His eyes never left mine, and I realized He was blessing me. I also was supremely conscious that I loved Him, and He loved me in a way that surpasses all human concept of the word love.

The next thing I knew, I was waking up very aware that I had met God. The experience is the most precious memory I have, and the details are still crystal clear to this day. He appeared to me in a way that matched with my belief system, but of course, He is absolute omnipotence, total energy, and can take on any form He wishes. I was just so happy I had made the right choice in deciding to ignore 'L and wait. It can sometimes, be a blessing, sometimes a curse, but we do have free will, and we can always choose God.

Meeting GOD While Sitting On A Cloud

My next meeting with God occurred Feb. 10th 6 a.m. 2009. It was such an incredible experience and so vivid that I was able to remember the details of the time and date.

I was in the middle stage and realized I had the opportunity to leave my body. As I did so, it soon became apparent that I was in a totally different dimension. I was in a pure white space, with high panorama windows at the far end. I gazed at the windows in awe. I couldn't wait to get to them and look out. I felt it was a passage to total freedom. I don't know where the feeling came from, but it was very real. This was not unique to my O.O.B.E., as on occasion, I sought a way to achieve total freedom, from gravity, from everything.

I ran towards the window and looked through and saw what I instinctively knew was part of heaven. Just outside, gathered in formation were the most beautiful, friendly clouds. They were in all kinds of different shapes and looked like cotton candy. There were a few white ones, but the majority were a beautiful petroleum blue, all against a white background.

This sight was so unreal, and welcoming. I couldn't wait to jump out and play.

Knowing that I was pure astral energy, I thought I could just go through the windows even though there was no visible means to open them. I tried to go through but realized that I couldn't. This was the first and only time I was unable to penetrate something which appeared to be physical. The realization hit me that I somehow had to open the window, but there was no visible mechanism. Without thinking, I touched the window and slid it open, to my complete surprise. I was ecstatic. Without hesitation, I leapt into the fluffy clouds. It was as if they were drawing me into them, and I couldn't wait. I jumped up and down and immersed myself in these magnificent clouds. I knew I was in heaven, and I had no intention of ever leaving, it was simply too marvelous.

Then I noticed a figure standing close to a larger than life building, too incredible to try and describe. I knew immediately that it was God.

He had taken on a human persona, to fit in with my idea of God, complete with a long, white beard. He was tall and had white hair and held a staff in His hand. He was waiting patiently for me, on a white cloud.

I spoke to Him and asked Him, "Will I make it as an actress?" I was really worried what His answer would be because it is my biggest life dream, that I had sacrificed everything for, and I didn't want to hear no. I would rather He said nothing, but to my complete surprise, He said, "Yes."

Immediately after He had spoken, I fell through the clouds and ended up back in the same room I had just left, longing to see God again. I leapt straight back through the window, which was already opened, and into the clouds. The feeling was fantastic; like nothing any earthly experience can come near. Sure enough, God was still there, patiently waiting for me. I asked him another question, but I don't recall what it was. God gave me an answer, but again, I don't recall.

No sooner had He answered, then I was back inside the same room for the second time.

Guess what. I wasn't going to stay there. Once again, I jumped through the window into the clouds. As I landed, I started walking towards God, who was patiently waiting for me. Again, I spoke with him. This time, I had a couple of questions that were so important to me, I had to have answers. The first question was "In all your other dimensions, apart from the human dimension, am I one of your archangels?" He looked at me very seriously and didn't answer, but I felt that it was so, but I wasn't supposed to ask. The second question, you may not be surprised to learn was "Will I become a recognized actress?" God looked at me again, showing no impatience. I still wasn't expecting a yes, but that's just me. I need confirmation before I believe anything. However, He smiled and said, "Yes you will." For the third time, I fell through the clouds, deliriously happy.

When I eventually ended up back in my body, I was so disappointed. I wanted to stay and talk to God, to ask Him more questions but I knew there would be other opportunities.

GOD Shows Me The Migration Of Souls

My next meeting with God came under the heading 'spectacular.' Even with the use of the most descriptive words in the English language it is difficult to give more than an impression of the magnificence that is God.

Once again, I was in the middle stage, and in another dimension. I was flying extremely quickly through a light fog. The air had no or little density. As I flew towards heaven, I could see around me flashes of lightning. I was concerned that the flashes of lightning would damage me, but I was able to fly right through it without any problems.

An outstanding memory is that as I was flying to heaven, all around me were humans, with astral bodies. I saw the bodies as dead, but I knew the souls were not dead, and were on their journey to heaven. The interesting thing was that I was witnessing all this, while still in my astral, human body, with an out of body experience. I believe God wanted me to see how souls went to heaven. I noticed that my speed had decreased to allow me to see the migration of souls, but once I had witnessed this, again I was traveling very fast and broke through into a place of extraordinary bright light that had a very peaceful essence. However, I could not see through the light, as it transformed into a maze.

As I was floating around in this white maze- like light, I felt lighter than air, the most amazing experience, all the while peace and tranquility enveloped me. I entered a large house and heard a voice. I followed the source of the voice and ended up in a room where the voice was coming from. I entered and saw a figure in front of me. I couldn't make out any details, but I just knew it was God. He was an opaque silhouette.

God spoke to me for a while and I didn't answer as I knew I had to listen. Later I realized that I was being given a message.

I was so disturbed by it that I'm still hesitant about writing it in its entirety, but I feel a responsibility to repeat it as I heard it.

God told me He has given up hope for mankind on planet earth. "Everyone will cease to exist due to natural disasters. The only reason this wild, unpredictable planet Earth was ever peaceful was because of my control over it. I will now give up and let go of control. The planet will run wild and constantly create and recreate natural disasters that will quickly destroy all mankind."

His voice became more powerful and deeper as he said, "I am giving up on mankind, they have greatly disappointed me. They are now on their own, left to their own destruction."

My take on God's message is not a revelation. We have constantly abused the gift of free will. We have killed, ignored, denied all of those who attempted to bring his message of love, kindness, forgiveness instead of greed, power, vanity, selfishness, and ego.

We kill each other in the name of religion. We decimate and pollute our planet as if we can throw it away and get a new one. We mindlessly waste more and more, while millions starve to death daily. We mistreat animals cruelly by killing mercilessly, and disrespecting those totally helpless creatures, the most innocent on our planet. They can't communicate by talking; they are defenseless and are constantly being abused. We must change our ways and start respecting these beautiful, innocent creatures by showing mercy and compassion.

THERE IS HOPE, but only if we evolve. We need to recognize that we are in a downward spiral, and to change that we must **START DOING THINGS FOR THE GREATER GOOD.**

Only then, when humanity acts, can we aspire to be the creatures worthy of God's love.

GOD Shows Me Archangel Gabriel

This experience is one that must be told, not for my benefit, but for everyone that reads this book. It is a direct message from God that cannot be ignored.

I was out of my body, yet again, but this time with a strong feeling that I must see God. I was in another dimension and traveling through different dimensions, as an invisible force pushed me onwards.

I had an overwhelming desire to find God and was aware that I was archangel Gabriel.

I came across a room with a very different kind of door. The door was alive. It was vibrating and banging, shaking, hammering like thunder, and moving. The handle was a round silver door-knob. I knew instinctively I had to open the door.

There were entities with negative energies outside the door, and they told me no one could open the door. Then something happened I wasn't expecting. I suddenly became aware of a large, full sized mirror. I approached the mirror and took a long, hard look at myself. The reflection that stared back at me was nothing short of astonishing. It was the archangel Gabriel! This was the first and only time, to this day, I had ever seen her.

The vision that looked back at me, was me, but it was not me, it was her. She was tanned, as if she had been exposed to sunlight, and involved in a battle, as she was wearing body armor in dark silver. She had long, black, wavy hair, down to her waist. She was very slender and extremely beautiful with long, enormous wings, made from white feathers. After seeing this vision, I went straight to the door which I had been told couldn't be opened, and with no effort whatsoever, turned the knob and the door opened.

I entered an area and was approached by a female angel. She looked at me and I unfolded my wings, by will, so she could see. She nodded and pointed to another door I had to go through. I went through the door into another space, and immediately felt the presence of God. He had taken a human form, so I would recognize him.

He was intently looking at a map, which displayed all the countries of the world. He was aware of my presence and spoke to me in a stern voice. "I am disappointed and saddened by the human being's behavior." He then started discussing with other angels that were present, where to create natural catastrophes, and how many, and how many people no longer needed to be part of the planet.

This is the core of the message from God. The more that humans' make the wrong choices, succumbing to greed, selfishness and evil, the more 'L' wins. He is winning by influencing free will in a negative way. The more people make the right and unselfish choices, by being compassionate towards each other, and forgiving, is when God wins, along with mankind.

CHAPTER 15

Meeting My Dad In Heaven

My father was always very dear to me. My love for him was, and still is, unconditional. He wasn't there much when I was growing up, because he was always busy with business projects, and in his free time really enjoyed playing bridge. As I grew older, things changed. My father created an empire within the commercial real estate market.

He built an amazing family mansion, which included separate living spaces for everyone, also his office. This meant I was able to spend a lot of time with him, to the extent I would often give my opinion, which he respected, although it's true to say we always argued, as I always stuck to my opinions. He confided in me and the relationship grew very close.

Eventually, my father bought a second home in Marbella, Spain and we would go there often, sometimes with my friends. I would always spend Christmas with my family, usually in Marbella. It was my favorite time.

In 2009, I was in Los Angeles, preparing to travel to Marbella for Christmas, when I received a phone call from my mother. She told me that my father had fallen and had been taken to the hospital in Marbella. I had difficulty understanding this as my father was in great shape and played golf every day. My mother said that the doctors believed he fell because he had a slipped disk. I immediately flew to Marbella, where my mother met me and took me to the hospital my father was in.

When we arrived at the hospital, we were told the same story, that a slipped disk had caused my father's fall, but I wasn't satisfied. I began questioning the doctor and eventually discovered that my father had prostate cancer that had migrated to his spine. When I found out, I knew there was no way I could tell my father the extent it had spread, but I had to tell him he had cancer, in order to arrange for chemotherapy treatment.

This was one of the hardest things I have had to do in my life. I went into my father's room and told him he had a little bit of cancer and we both agreed to start the treatment. However, I knew it was a long shot, but so desperately wanted to believe he could be cured.

My mother and I returned to the hospital on a daily- basis and just before Christmas made plans to bring my father home for the holidays. When we had finished the arrangements, we returned home, and just as we arrived, received a phone call from the hospital to say my father had lapsed into a coma. We immediately drove back to the hospital, and I remember, to this day, it was the 22nd of December 2009.

As I stood at the end of the hospital bed, I simply could not accept he was in a coma, and approached him and said, "Dad, you need to wake up, wake up." To the amazement of everyone in the room, including doctors, my father answered me with a very stern voice. "Simona, do not wake me up." I knew I had to respect his wish, so I went back to the end of the bed, and with tears streaming down my face, I cried out to God. "Please take me instead, do not take my father. Why would you take my father? He loves life so much. Please take me instead because I'm not too fond of this life." At this point, he stopped breathing and I had to leave the room. I knew he was leaving his body. Christmas was never the same again. My love for him was so strong and has remained that way to this day, I still haven't gotten over it.

Meeting My Dad

Several days after my father passed, I had an out of body experience. I found myself in another dimension. It was a place full of turmoil and not of peace. I looked around and saw my father, walking around in a wasteland. I ran to him and grabbed him and told him strongly that he must leave this place and go directly to God. I felt he was in the 'in between place'. I led him over onto steady ground and took a good look at him. To my surprise, he looked good. Like a younger version of himself. I stretched my arms to an almost twilight looking sky and told him that he had to go through a specific point in the sky. As my arms raised, I parted the sky and a crack appeared full of white light. My father saw the white light and at that point, I was taken back into my body.

Meeting My Dad A Second Time

Within a couple of days of my out of body experience, when I was taken to meet my father, I was once again transported to the same place. To my amazement, my father was still there. He had not done what I had told him to do on my previous visit. I went straight to him and in a very stern voice said, "You must go to God now." Once again, I stretched out both arms and parted the skies of heaven. This time it became a totally open gateway. Thankfully, he was now drawn to God's white light, and I knew at this point he was on his way to the right place, God's home. I was then taken back into my body.

<u>Testing GOD-To See My Father</u>

After the passing of my father, I stayed in Marbella for quite a while with my mother. She comforted me as best she could, but I was inconsolable.

Early in the morning of January 5th, I was in bed, and I found myself in the middle stage, very close to full consciousness. I could hear my mother in an adjacent room, speaking on the phone. I suddenly felt, and heard, a vibrating sound, and something started massaging my body. As usual, I felt no fear, but made the conscious decision to allow it to continue, to discover what or who was massaging me. Without warning, I felt a body cozying up to me. I immediately knew the presence was not God like. But, as I'm curious and totally without fear, I allowed it to lift me up, then it hit me. I suddenly knew without a doubt it was 'L.'

I understood he was trying to imitate 'divine energy' and 'levitation,' which could only come from God. He was trying to mislead me, but there is a huge difference. He is not capable of creating the divine sensation because he is not divine, but dark. He told me several times that he loved me, but I knew it was him. As this was happening, I was in between dimensions but conscious of everything around me.

He then took me to another dimension, to a much bigger room, with a huge bed. Once again, he attempted to seduce my soul, so I asked him, "Do you love God?" He didn't answer. I asked him again, "Do you love God?" and I stated that "I love God," over and over. I wouldn't stop telling him that I loved God. This made him very frustrated and he blurted out, "Why do you love God, since God will do nothing for you." I answered, "Let it come to a test. I will call God, and if God comes to me, it surely means he loves me." This made him irritated, as he already knew the answer. I yelled as loud as I could. "God if you love me, you must prove it now." As soon as I had stopped yelling, an opening appeared in the wall of the big, spacious room, and a parade of God's light beings and angels, entered. The angels had big, beautiful white wings and the light beings looked like people, but they were made from translucent light. They gathered around, placing their hands on me in a protective circle and willed 'L' out of the room.

I asked them if I could see my father. This caused great debate among them. Finally, quite a few human people entered the room. I knew immediately they had already passed on. Among them, I recognized my grandfather, but to my great disappointment, my father was not there. I was devastated. I screamed, yelled and cried to God. "I want to see my father." I was very aware that no one alive on earth had been able to cross to the place where people who have passed are. This place is another section of a completely different dimension that is a part of Heaven.

The sincerity of my pain and agonizing cries to God were being heard. They granted me access, but only for a short moment they said, as I was quickly transported to the place where my father was. I was in front of a restaurant in this other dimension, and I knew everyone in the place had already passed. They told me to enter and look to the left, my father would be there. I entered the restaurant and saw a round table to my left and there he was, enjoying himself. He was looking the way he did when he was at his best, and how I remembered him in his late thirties. He was thrilled to see me, and stood to greet and hug me, and I could feel his love for me.

I said, "Dad, I am not dead, but have been allowed to visit you by God. I need to know how you are. I miss you and love you." He smiled at me, without a worry on his smooth face. I then said, "I can't stay long," but he was also in a hurry. "I have things to do," he said. "I am quite busy." He seemed very happy and content. Suddenly I was removed from the place, and back in my bed, and back in my body.

During this out of body experience I was totally aware of my mother's voice in the next room. This was so amazing to me that I asked her if she had been on the phone, and of course, she confirmed she had been.

Postscript

The astonishing thing is, that after my screaming session with God, and even more so after I started writing this book, I have been granted access to see my father in the dimension where those that have passed are, which is a part of heaven.

Went To Heaven To Visit My Dad

Around 5-5:45 a.m., I had the most amazing experience with my father. I was out of my body, strangely enough, without going through the usual stage. I was in another dimension, in a room, very light, everything was white, and I was sitting on the bed. Suddenly a man appeared, with two white towels over his head, and lay next to me on the floor. I asked, "Who are you?" He laughed out loud in a really loving way. I sat down next to him and peeled the towels off his head. Underneath the towels I saw the face of my father, just not quite as I remembered him, but I knew it was my father. I had never seen my father look like this. He was probably in his early twenties, but I recognized his bone structure and eyes immediately.

The biggest difference was his hair, which was slicked back in an Elvis type style, and some fell forward over his face. He started laughing again and said, "Yes, Simona, it's me." I said, "Dad, dad, where are you exactly in heaven?" He said, "I'm on this level in heaven, come on, I'll show you." He took me outside the room into a huge space, with green grass everywhere, and many white buildings. Lots of people were interacting like normal people, and then within a split second we were back in the room.

I took another look at my dad. He looked astonishing, so young, so happy, so full of life. I started bombarding him with questions. "What's it like being here in heaven? Do you remember anything about earth? Does anyone at this level in heaven remember anything about their lives on earth?" He replied, "Yes, we all do remember earth, but it's not important anymore." I said, "But dad, do you remember all you accomplished on earth?" I then started showing him pictures of himself, our family, and all the grand real estate he developed. I had no idea where the pictures came from, I just had them. I said, "You were so accomplished, so successful, everyone recognized and respected you, don't you remember that?" He didn't respond. I said, "Dad, what about me? I miss you, and I love you, and I can't wait to see you again, I want to be with you." He said, "But Simona, you may not end up in the same place as I am because you're one of God's favorites." I couldn't believe he said that, and I asked, "What do you mean?" He said, "God loves you very, very much, so you may end up on a whole different level than where I am."

The way that he said that, as a matter of fact, made me want to ask him how he knew I was one of God's favorites, what was that level like, what did he know about it. I was bursting with questions, and we kept on talking about things which I can't remember. Again, I told him all about himself and life on earth. He had it as a memory, but his memory was vague. I kept on reminding him how grand he had been on earth.

As you can imagine, this was one of the most emotional experiences I've ever had, and I so wanted to stay with him, and not go back.

I also asked my dad if he remembered that I had to take him to God.

I woke up but couldn't wait to go back to sleep again, I so wanted to be with him always.

CHAPTER 16

Archangel Gabriel-Sodom And Gomorrah

<u>Gabriel</u>

This chapter was challenging to write, as it describes in depth my relationship with archangel Gabriel. How it began, what it could mean and how it continues. I have used all my ability, my memory, experiences, and understanding of what is a complex string of events that eventually led me to the conclusion that many times, Gabriel has merged with me (my astral body). This would happen when out of my body, and in another dimension, but I was totally aware of it.

I realized that what I'm about to describe will border on the fantastic, to most people, and so, you can imagine how I felt, trying to deal with this amazing phenomenon. I must emphasize here, that in no way do I claim to walk around every day, thinking I'm an angel with wings. Oh no! I would be carted away with those kinds of claims. However, when I am out of my body, and in another dimension, the experiences I have are very real, just a million times more exciting.

So, with all of this in mind, I beg you to suspend your disbelief, if only for a while, and take on board the message, and don't be too hard on this humble messenger. We are all on the same journey. Let's listen to each other with an open mind.

The first time that I became aware of the name archangel Gabriel, was in L.A., when I was channeling and speed writing. At first, it was just the name, which didn't mean much to me at that time, but then I began to receive messages, both from her and about her. One specific message, that stood out, stated that Gabriel was the only archangel amongst the archangel hierarchy that consisted of female energy.

I was so amazed and curious about the fact that she was the only female archangel that I was desperate for confirmation and began serious research.

I systematically checked out Google, libraries and book- stores, searching for any information that I could find about her. I became so obsessive that I wouldn't give up and eventually came across just two sources of information, among hundreds of searches, that confirmed Gabriel was in fact a female archangel.

Surprise, surprise, I still didn't quite believe the messages I was receiving and decided to seek more proof. I turned to my tarot cards, making sure I used a new set. The deck contained 78 individual cards, every one different. My way of reading the cards, which was very unusual, was to ask a question while shuffling the deck.

On this occasion, I asked for confirmation that the messages from archangel Gabriel were real. The queen or princess of cups would leap out every time. I repeated the process hundreds of times over a period of years, just to make sure, and on every occasion, one of those two cards would pop out. This phenomenon was witnessed many times by different people.

While all this was going on, I was continuing to have O.O.B.E. always ending up in other dimensions, where I would grow archangel wings and feel archangel Gabriel merge with my astral body. Ironically, I still couldn't believe what I was experiencing and used every opportunity when I was in other dimensions to ask, "What is my name?" Without exception, every entity greeted me with, "Hi, Gabriel." Somewhere, deep down, at an early point, I knew Gabriel was real, and that we merged when I entered other dimensions, but the humanness in me had difficulty accepting what I was experiencing. I'm sure if you were me, you would have similar reservations. Knowing me, I couldn't let things rest just there, I had to know more about Gabriel, so I started asking God by channeling. Also, at the same time, I received information freely.

I formed a couple of fundamental ideas, that run contrary to popular religious beliefs. Gabriel was infatuated with Lucifer when he was in heaven and was devastated when God ordered Michael to cast him out.

Gabriel argued with Lucifer when he fought against God, and always remained faithful and loyal to God (except for one occasion), as she loved him like a father. She was heartbroken when Lucifer was thrown out.

Lucifer was God's favorite before he started the rebellion, and was the most beautiful of all the angels, so when Michael was ordered along with other angels, who all favored God, to throw Lucifer out, along with his followers, Michael was happy to have Gabriel to himself. She was the most beautiful female angel, and was upset with God, so much so that God made her part of his covenant between good and evil.

God allowed Gabriel to descend to Earth, but He had already chosen a specific female with a pure soul, whenever Gabriel took human form.

They would become two in one, and she would be able to witness for herself if the choices Lucifer made to tempt mankind were fundamentally wrong. She soon realized that Lucifer's sole intent was to spite God as much as possible.

However, there was another big reason why Gabriel was allowed by God to occupy a specific human soul, whenever she chose to.

Sodom and Gomorrah

As I learned more about Gabriel, I discovered that there was one occasion where she directly disobeyed God. It happened when God was displeased with human- kind's behavior, in the cities of Sodom and Gomorrah. They had succumbed to the temptations of greed, violence, selfishness, and did absolutely nothing for the greater good.

God ordered two of his most trusted archangels, one of whom was Gabriel, to descend to earth to see to it that the cities of Sodom and Gomorrah were destroyed. However, Gabriel's compassion for the human species made her hesitate. She realized that she was not capable of participating in such an act of destruction, so great was her compassion for humans.

She decided to abandon the mission and returned to heaven. Needless to say Sodom and Gomorrah was destroyed anyway, as it was God's will. After Gabriel's return to heaven, God called upon her, as He was extremely displeased with her disobedience. God was so angry with her that He removed her from her post, as one of the most trusted archangels.

To Gabriel's relief, the removal from her post, and God's wrath, was only temporary.

However, God decided to teach Gabriel a lesson. God spoke to her and said, "My verdict is that in order for you to understand that my will must be obeyed, since only I know the truth of what will and shall play out in all eternity, is that you will experience suffering as humans do. You will become part of a human body for as long as I decide. Life in a human body comes with suffering, amongst other sensations, and because of your passion for humans' and their nature, you will now experience, what you have for so long longed for; life in a human body."

Eventually God relented and gave Gabriel permission to come and go into a human body, as she wished.

After having this information channeled down to me, over and over, I decided to seek confirmation and started researching.

Despite every effort on my part, I failed to uncover any collaborative information, until one day, my ex and I took a trip to Port Townsend in Washington. We were visiting some of his family members and I needed to figure out where the place was, as I had never heard of it.

We arrived with some time to kill, so we wandered around the small town. I spotted a quaint old bookstore and went inside to browse. To this day, I still have no idea how all this happened, but I stumbled across a rare book, lodged on a shelf, almost out of reach. It was a book about angels, and of course, I skimmed through it. To my utter amazement, I came across a passage that precisely described archangel Gabriel's removal from her post, due to her disobedience towards God, when she did not follow his will to destroy Sodom and Gomorrah. I was astonished to further learn that she had later been reinstated to her post.

CHAPTER 17

War In Heaven

As has been stated before on many occasions, the first war in heaven took place because of Lucifer's envy of God's creation of us as human beings.

God had such love for his creation that he created us in his image, meaning, we all have a soul and that soul is God. Lucifer's envy caused him to rebel against God and he was not alone. He had an army of rebel angels (known as demons on earth), all wanting to fight God, because of their jealousy of God's love for human beings.

When Lucifer was cast out, along with his rebel angels, he became vindictive, and his sole purpose since then has been to pollute God's most loved creations, the human species. In order to get back at God, Lucifer has found ways to tempt humans and appeal to the dark side of their nature by tempting mankind to use free will in all the wrong ways. This has created chaos among the human species. Instead of man choosing to do things for the greater good, he has been drawn in a different direction from what God's original intent was. Man has succumbed to greed, selfishness, and ego, and has forgotten how to show compassion.

Simultaneously, as Lucifer continues to pollute the human species, a second war in heaven is taking place. When I refer to heaven, I'm not referring to the heaven you and I gaze upon. I'm referring to one of the many other dimensions in which heaven exists.

In this second war for heaven, Lucifer, along with his rebel angels, persist in his fight against God. He's fighting God for the ultimate purpose of taking charge of heaven, which, (in his demented mind) he believes can only be done, if he creates absolute turmoil as he misleads the human species in every possible way.

As I stated before, the methods he uses to manipulate us, is by tempting us to abuse our free will. It's up to us as humans, to resist the temptations and change our ways, by doing things for the greater good, instead of only focusing on our own selfish needs.

Because of Lucifer's conviction that the human species is too vain to change their ways, he continues to fight God on the sole premise that God's experiment with his beloved humans will fail. In Lucifer's mind, he believes that he is God's adversary, as he is trying to take control of heaven. He will, however, never succeed at this, as God is way too strong and powerful, the creator of everything that exists, including Lucifer himself.

However, Lucifer continues to fight along with his rebel angels against God, and his faithful loyal angels. I can attest to this as I was part of a specific battle in one of my O.O.B.E. I had an encounter with God, prior to the battle, which I will now describe.

Encounter With GOD

In this O.O.B.E, I did something which I normally don't care to do. The urge to leave this dimension is so powerful that I can't wait to get out, but on this occasion, I looked back. I saw myself still lying in bed. I turned around and stood right next to my bed knowing I was out of my body. I noticed that I was lying on my right side. I was still wearing the purple, long sleeved blouse I had put on the night before going to bed. I felt happy to be out of my body and experiencing total freedom from physical matter. Free from the laws of gravity that binds us to the planet.

I quickly escaped into another dimension, pursuing the one entity I desire to be close to; God. I ended up in an enormous white room. I stood at one end and at the other end, I clearly saw God, who had taken on his human shape, so I would recognize him. He stood looking at me very intensely and completely silent. He was very serious. I opened my mouth, as I always do, as I tend to talk too much, according to other people, and was just about to speak to God and pose one of my thousand questions, when bang, out of nowhere, I was whisked back into my body again.

I wondered, "Why wasn't I able to speak to Him?" and "Why was God so serious as He was looking at me?"

After my next out of body experience, I discovered why God was so serious.

Angel War-Captured And Escape

I was out of my body, with my great white angel wings attached on my back. The wings were so huge that they were the wings of an archangel. I knew it was Gabriel.

I was flying very high in the heavens, as I suddenly saw a host of other angels, with black wings flying towards me.

One, the biggest of the unfriendly angels with enormous black wings, flew directly at me and hovered in front of me, as all the others, and there were many, formed a circle round me. I was trapped. I knew I was in trouble because for some reason, God wasn't there to protect me and help me by shining His golden light.

The big archangel with the enormous black wings was of course 'L.'

"Now I have you, archangel." These were his words to me; and he did!

I was captured and taken to a 'house' in another dimension.

There I was tortured but didn't know this until I woke up. I had been asleep during the extremely grotesque torture I had endured. 'L' showed me pictures of all the angels with black wings torturing me, and I felt sick to my stomach. I was chained, beaten and abused in every possible way. They took me to a room to hold me captive. I knew there was only one way to escape…to convince one of the rebel angels who hadn't been totally polluted with evil yet, to help me. But I needed to trick this angel to show me the way out of 'L's' dimension, which was unfathomable.

I found an angel, that was curious about me anyway, and hoped it was open to persuasion. I asked it, nonchalantly if there was a way out of the 'house,' and it answered "Yes, of course, but it is difficult and complicated." We communicated telepathically. I asked if it could show me, just for fun, and it said, "Yes, why not."

I followed it and to say it was complicated was an understatement. We had to go through walls, doors, windows, and secret passages, and every time I believed I was out, and saw the blue heaven above me it was fake. I was still trapped. I felt hopeless.

Finally, as I was about to give up, I was suddenly out. I felt exhilarated.

I thanked the angel who had shown me the way, and to this day I am still wondering why it had helped me escape. Strangely enough, it seemed pleased to do so.

"Did God, after all, have a finger in play here?" I flew as high as I could up into the heavens, and I was free. I turned around and saw a large group of angels flying towards me, all big, with huge white wings.

I started screaming an angel scream. I had never heard a sound like this before, all the angels started flying directly towards me. Some screamed back. They could tell that I was lost. As we greeted, I told my story and prepared them for what would follow. Black angels would be searching for me, trying to find me, and they did.

Picture the scene. A huge crowd of angels with black wings on one side, and all my angels on the other side, and I was in the middle.

Then it started. A war, so horrible, that I simply cannot describe it. All I know is that I started fighting like the warrior angel I had been so many times before.

The white angels against the dark angels. It was a long, exhausting battle. Suddenly, it was over. I stood there, a victory on our behalf, and I looked directly at 'L' and said. "I beat you again." He, along with all his rebel angels disappeared.

We had won. I flew among all the angels with big white wings and rejoiced that we were yet again a team. We flew towards God's 'home.'

CHAPTER 18

My Apocalyptic Vision-
June 23ʳᵈ 2018

This chapter was extraordinarily difficult to write. The content of the message was so disturbing, I was apprehensive about passing it on, but quickly realized I didn't have a choice. Throughout the book I have been faithful to God's messages. I felt a huge responsibility to record every word, literally, and let others judge the content. I ask only, that you bear in mind that I am just the messenger, as I relay this apocalyptic vision of how the future may unfold, unless we act now to curb our greedy, power seeking nature, and evolve to who we truly are, children of God.

I was at home in Los Angeles, in bed in the morning when I felt the Christ energy infuse my body. Every cell was in a state of ecstasy. I levitated and found myself standing in my bedroom, looking at my physical body. I was completely aware that I was out of my body. Instantly I was transported by an invisible force to another place. I knew, without knowing how I knew, that I was in the future. I was witnessing a war. Asian troops were attacking another country in order to gain territory. I spoke with an Asian woman who was in charge and asked her, "Why is this horrific war happening?" She answered, "The leader ordered the attack."

I explained "It is totally unnecessary to have all these wars, among human beings, and for what? To acquire more territory?" To my surprise, she told me she understood exactly what I meant. She said, "Tell every leader your point of view."

As I stood there with her, I willfully unfolded my archangel wings and flew up high in the sky to overview the planet earth. What I saw was absolutely devastating. I saw massive warfare everywhere, natural catastrophes, big trains sliding off bridges into the sea, earthquakes, etc. Everything was chaos because of human greed and destruction.

I was witnessing events taking place in the future. The world was in chaos, and maybe coming to an end, all because of the human species greed for power. I flew higher and saw an enormous earthquake which forced another train into the sea. I immediately understood what was happening. People had gone too far. I knew the earthquake would create a massive tsunami, beyond the scope of imagination, big enough to cover most of the earth.

I flew even higher into the sky, but not high enough to totally avoid the tsunami. It grew beyond comprehension in the oceans and headed towards land. I knew I had to fly 'home.' I kept on flying up into the heavens, but the wave was so gigantic that I hit it, but had no fear and kept on flying through it. Finally, I reached a point where I was free of it and on my way up to heaven. I flew higher and higher with great speed and force.

Suddenly I saw the sun. It was enormous, much bigger than I had ever seen it on earth, but it didn't burn me. As I flew closer, I was shown the gate to paradise. I was being shown the gate, in order to know the exact place to enter another dimension where paradise lay. I was given a vision of the gate to paradise as I had never seen it before. I knew I had to fly through this specific space and into God's paradise where I was expected, as I had been called home.

The gate and its surroundings were breathtakingly beautiful. It is impossible to describe with words. It was gold and the colors around it were all delicate pastel, unreal in their exquisite beauty.

The gate was open, waiting for me. However, I had been delayed because of the tsunami, and the gate started closing.

As I continuously watched the gate closing, I increased my speed to the limit, and just as I thought I couldn't make it, I threw myself through the tiny opening, right before it closed. I had made it!

On the other side was God's magnificent kingdom, paradise, and the archangel's headquarters. I entered the archangel's headquarters which was a massive, white building that consisted of many smaller ones. I approached one of the archangels and asked him where I could find God, having just arrived from earth and returned home. He pointed to a regular chamber which I entered and found God. He had taken a human form, and was leaning back on a sofa, in deep thought. I sat next to Him and we had one of our 'conversations.' I asked questions, and God answered, explaining everything to me.

I had been called from earth as it would cease to exist as we know it. The human' race would become extinct and there was no more need for me there. The world would lie 'in rest' for millions of years and then, at a certain point, life in its smallest form, would start again, as several times before. Again, humans, with their free will had chosen to use it for greed, power, and all the wrong reasons.

CHAPTER 19

Who Or What Is GOD?

Most people have their own idea of what or who God is, based on religious upbringing, cultural influences, exposure to environmental experiences or in many cases, a belief or no belief system they have adopted. What I am about to relate comes as a direct channeling message from God, given to me at 3:28 am in the morning of July 18, 2018. I was awoken with a blinding migraine. As messages came tumbling down, I grabbed my tape recorder and recorded the following, totally verbatim.

GOD

I am an energy that has always existed even before I decided to create all the universes. Even though human beings physically have only mathematically and scientifically measured one universe, you know that there are many more. One going into another; it is a never-ending process. And considering that you only use up to 10% of your brain, you're not capable of understanding the mathematics of the universes that I've created. The mathematics are very different from your earthly calculations. There are so many concepts and so many phenomena that you still do not understand. Like what are black holes, and how is it possible to travel through a worm hole?

You, however, are not physically capable of doing this. Only pure energy can do it and not be harmed, except there are other beings in my other universes so highly evolved that they have material that can bend and are not harmed by traveling through worm holes, which is how those beings are visiting planet earth.

I've always existed ever since you believed time began. There is no time with me, never has been, never will be. Know that only when you are pure astral energy, as human beings, are you able to access my many other countless dimensions.

So, as I said there is no time, the only reason why human beings have created time going back to the Mayans and before, has to do with the expiration date of your physical bodies. Your physical body is only able to live for so long, but you never really die. Your soul, which is immortal, is part of my energy. That is what I have granted every human being, a touch of me, a little part of my energy, which is what you call the soul. So, we know that when the soul leaves the body whether it may be by passing on or having an out of body experience, it consists of all knowledge that we normally would believe to be perceived or contained within the brain.

All memory, everything from that lifetime of a person, is in that soul. But that's only a fraction of what's in the soul. There is me in the soul, and I am everything that ever has been, and everything there ever will be. I have dwelled in an empty space for so long, before I decided to create the first universe, and kept on expanding. I dwelled in chaos. You believed there was nothing and then the big bang happened, but the big bang was just a fraction of a little incident. There was pure chaos. I simply decided to put order into that chaos, which I did by creating the big bang. You see how perfect the planets in your solar system are aligned. How perfectly far the sun is from the earth, not able to burn you. How the moon affects the tide, how everything is impeccable. That is my creation. I am everything, I am the alpha and the omega. I have always been and will always be.

You, however, will not be able to perceive this concept of infinity. You may mathematically have a formula of how you measure infinity, but you are simply not capable of understanding it. I have always been, I will always be, and I shall be forever. That is something that human beings can simply not perceive because of limited access to the brain, which is what processes information. But when you are only soul, and you have access to me, you completely understand everything.

So, you call me God? I guess that's as good a name as any. She's calling me God. That's not a problem. I am an energy source with all knowledge of everything. I have the capability of creating anything and everything I wish, and I have the capability of destroying it. I am not all peaceful as there is chaos in many of the other universes. There is still some chaos in your universe. There is chaos on your planet. And even though I am an energy full of love, which is why I created my son, who only had my energy and so much of it, and had direct access to me, I could see what was being done with my creation, my son!

I am not too pleased with the way human beings are abusing their free will. But then again, you are only a small fraction of what I have created. There are many other species in the countless other universes, as I said before. And yes, they have been to earth. And yes, some people are aware of them. Most of them are peaceful as they are highly evolved, and with evolvement comes the concept of non-destruction and peace, and the desire to exist.

With little evolvement, which is what humans have, the knowledge simply isn't there. There is only self-destructive behavior. All the fundamental flaws of humanity as mentioned before. Greed, hunger for more power, always for more. Did you ever consider that you cannot take any of your accumulated material possessions with you? When you leave, you leave as being only soul!

So, all these highly intelligent beings I created long before I ever created you, have a different concept of what it means to live in peace, but then again, they are not all non-hostile. There are some that try to dominate others, so some of them are not perfect either. And what is perfection, anyway?

The reason I created my son, Jesus, was because of a passion for the human species, as I had given them part of my force, and everyone, the soul. I created him to spread messages of love, forgiveness, understanding, living in co-existence, accepting each other, no matter who you are. I am not really one of you, even though I am. By having a slight little essence of me in each of you, I see you and I feel you.

So, by my son spreading these messages, it obviously worked for some that did become very evolved. There are some of you human beings that are very evolved and do understand this. Most of you, however, didn't and still don't. My son didn't stand a chance, but he was willing to make the ultimate sacrifice in order to spread my message, which is love and understanding. As I said before, he was willing to die for you, something that I did not appreciate because did you really earn that? How far have you come since then? What does your world look like now? How have you evolved? Some of you have, but few.

Yes, you have bettered your mathematical skills, and skills in physics and science, but with the capability of only being able to access around 10% of your brain, when you have access to 100% it is only a small fraction isn't it?

And let me tell you, if you did have access to 100%, which you only do in a couple of instances when you're not in your physical body anymore, and not dependent on your brain as a filter that absorbs, dissects and tries to understand, you would be pure energy and not capable of being in your body. You would not want to be in your body. There would be an explosion of the soul leaving the body. You would want to go back to the ultimate source itself, which is me, God, and become one with me.

You human beings are here just a fraction of time, which you estimate according to your expiration date. You're here and then you're gone. Generation upon generation. I, however, shall always exist.

Look upon this and remember. There is no time in any of my universes or dimensions. There are occurrences. You are, however, a victim of time because of the way I designed you. Your matter does expire, but your soul is immortal and shall come back to me, as I am God.

GOD-Messages

1) You never really die. It is merely a transition.

2) You will become part of me and will be reunited with all your loved ones who have made this transition.

3) It is said that before the big bang, there was nothing. But that isn't so. I was always there. My energy filled all and then I created your universe, solar system, and you.

4) My will is superior to anything in existence and will determine who will come back to me.

5) You assume you use 10% of your brain capacity, but each of you are different. Some use more, some less.

6) The brain is merely an organ. The soul is the key. The soul is pure energy which is divine and consists of all knowledge.

7) (The author's personal message to the reader):

I am the messenger, and I am not a scientist, nor a mathematician or physicist. I simply write from the experiences I've had during the past twenty years, and from God channeling through me.

GOD Speaks

And again, you start the cycle. It is merely a repetition of what already was many times until you self-destructed.

How far will you go this time, humans? Will you evolve, or self-destruct again?

So many other species I created have evolved far beyond you. They are the ones visiting you. You have named them 'extra-terrestrials.' Most of them live in peace and harmony. They watch you and await, and so do I. Maybe this time, you will be able to access more knowledge, which equals peace, and not live in ignorance, which equals destruction.

Every time evolved beings try to connect as they have on multiple occasions with my messenger, even shown themselves, she was without fear and curious and accepting. You, however, always rush to an assumption that they are hostile. What if they are not? They helped you before to evolve thousands of years ago (keep the pyramids in Egypt in mind). The Egyptians especially got help from higher evolved species that amongst other things, helped build the pyramids.

The secret lies within your brain being able to access more of the ultimate knowledge your soul consists of. The soul is my essence. You have, however, not recognized the connection. Only when you leave your physical body, shall you return to me. Your consciousness will be complete. It will be me.

If you could reach a point where your vibrational energy evolved and became more consciously part of me, you would have significantly evolved.

Your brain is a super- computer. Only with that can you access part of the knowledge in your soul as you're in your physical body. Feeling trapped? Leave your body and you are immediately 100% of everything, part of me, as I am everything and everywhere.

Time for you, due to your physical body's expiration date is of the essence. That is all you have, time. Are you using it wisely?

Instead of constantly being consumed with accumulating more material things, more power, and succumbing to greed, try to learn, study, and evolve as a species. But then again, I may be speaking to a lot of deaf ears. Am I? Remember, once leaving the physical body, time simply ceases to exist. And your essence becomes part of me. Know that past, present, and future, all simultaneously co-exist in my other parallel dimensions.

CHAPTER 20

GOD's Message To Lucifer

During the early part of May 2019, I began to receive channeled messages from God. The content of the messages was so far reaching and awesome to contemplate, that I could hardly wait for 'L' to show up and pass on God's words. As the days wore on, the messages became more frequent and more intense, to the extent I felt I had to share with someone. A trusted friend came to the rescue and listened as I told him that God wanted me to pass on a specific message to Lucifer, the next time he made contact.

"God wants you to be a middleman between Him and 'L' Wow! Have you any idea how much God must trust you?"

I must say, I hadn't thought of it that way, but quickly realized the truth in my friend's words. I was so humbled. On the one hand I felt hugely privileged, but on the other the awesome responsibility was a heavy load to carry, and I had no idea when 'L' would show up.

I needn't have worried. On the night of May 22nd, early hours of May 23rd, he made his appearance. I was alone in my bedroom and soon found myself in the middle stage. Immediately I was whisked into another dimension, and as a matter of fact, into another bed. I remember noting it was made from wood and was covered with white sheets. I wasn't there long before I became aware of a presence in the room, so it was no surprise when I felt the covers being gently lifted and a body drew close to me and held me tightly. I knew right away that it was 'L'.

At that point in my spiritual journey, I was surprised to realize that I had compassion even for 'L' and as I turned to look at him, I felt a calmness come over me, knowing the message I had to relay was so important. His eyes were yellow, and his appearance was handsome, as he had been on the numerous occasions we had met in the past. He looked deeply into my eyes, as if he knew I had an important message for him, so I gently said, "Lucifer can I ask you a question about God.?"

To my utter amazement he said yes. At this point I must point out that 'L' spoke to me, and I responded using normal words, which was highly unusual, as in previous meetings, we had used thought transference, so I said,

"Lucifer, do you remember how you used to be in Heaven? Not only were you God's favorite archangel, but also the most beautiful, so God named you Lucifer, which means 'the bearer of light'. Remember you had the brightest light of all the archangels in Heaven, and God was most proud of you.

Then there was the rebellion. Why, Lucifer, why? Aren't you tired of being in the earthly realm? People are fully capable of abusing their free will without any help from you. Don't you want to go back to Heaven? Ask God's forgiveness so you can return to your former glory. Isn't that what you are really longing for?" 'L' didn't answer. I felt a compelling need to repeat the message, so I said, "Lucifer, please ask for God's forgiveness, that's all you have to do. God will forgive you. Remember your time in Heaven… remember your beauty…your glory. Don't you want to go back?"

The room went all quiet as I waited patiently for a response from Lucifer. His reaction astounded me. He looked at me with a depth of sadness in his eyes that was unfathomable, got up and silently left the room.

As soon as Lucifer disappeared, I got up and opened a door which led to an adjacent room. The light was dim, so I couldn't see much, but I stood in the center of the room and called out "God, are you there, can you hear me, is it o.k. what I said?

I knew I had conveyed the right message, but I desperately needed God's approval. Suddenly the room opened, and streams of incredible light poured in. As I stood bathed in this intense, wonderful light, a myriad of angels came towards me. They were of every shape and size imaginable. I was overwhelmed with a feeling of the purest love. Just when I thought my amazement couldn't reach any higher, I saw God walking towards me. I knew beyond doubt it was His way of confirming that I had done exactly as I had been asked.

God was wearing all white and had taken the shape and form that I would recognize, even though I know that God's essence is pure energy.

THE END